BELIZE

WESTVIEW PROFILES • NATIONS OF CONTEMPORARY LATIN AMERICA
Ronald M. Schneider, Series Editor

† *Nicaragua: The Land of Sandino*, Second Edition, Revised and Updated, Thomas W. Walker

† *Mexico: Paradoxes of Stability and Change*, Daniel Levy and Gabriel Székely

† *The Dominican Republic: A Caribbean Crucible*, Howard J. Wiarda and Michael J. Kryzanek

Colombia: Portrait of Unity and Diversity, Harvey F. Kline

† *Cuba: Dilemmas of a Revolution*, Juan M. del Aguila

Guatemala: A Nation in Turmoil, Peter Calvert

Puerto Rico, Pamela S. Falk

Bolivia: Land of Struggle, Waltraud Queiser Morales

Belize: A New Nation in Central America, O. Nigel Bolland

Ecuador, William Schodt

Honduras: Caudillo Politics and Military Rulers, James A. Morris

Paraguay, Riordan Roett

Uruguay, Martin Weinstein

† Available in hardcover and paperback.

About the Book and Author

Independent from Britain only since 1981, the new nation of Belize is situated at the intersection of two cultural spheres: the English-speaking Afro-Caribbean countries and the Spanish-speaking Central American republics. Its scanty population of about 150,000 is culturally heterogeneous, and its various ethnic groups coexist in a complex pattern of social, economic, and political interactions.

This profile of Belize provides a general introduction to both the historical background and the contemporary status of this microstate. Professor Bolland examines the processes of change currently taking place in Belize, including the increasing influence of the United States in the region, the danger of Belize's involvement in the expanding Central American conflicts, and the influx of refugees into Belize from these conflicts. He traces the major shifts in the economy that have occurred since World War II, as well as recent developments in consumption patterns, communications, trade unions, and government economic policies. The emergence and culmination of Belize's independence movement are explored in light of the country's internal politics and regional relations with other Commonwealth Caribbean nations and the Central American republics. The book concludes with an evaluation of Belize's problems and an assessment of its prospects for the future.

O. Nigel Bolland is professor of sociology and chairperson of the Department of Sociology and Anthropology at Colgate University, Hamilton, New York.

To the working people who created Belize,
and especially to the children who will inherit it,
with respect

BELIZE

A New Nation in
Central America

O. Nigel Bolland

Westview Press / Boulder and London

Westview Profiles/Nations of Contemporary Latin America

Published in 1986 in the United States of America by Westview Press, Inc.; Frederick A. Praeger, Publisher; 5300 Central Avenue, Boulder, Colorado 80301

Library of Congress Cataloging-in-Publication Data
Bolland, O. Nigel.
  Belize, a new nation in Central America.
  (Westview profiles. Nations of contemporary Latin
America)
  Bibliography: p.
  Includes index.
  1. Belize. I. Title. II. Series.
F1443.B65 1985   972.82   85-20385
ISBN 0-8133-0005-3

Printed and bound in the United States of America

10   9   8   7   6   5   4   3   2   1

Contents

vii

Tables and Illustrations

ix

Foreword

Latin America, although overwhelmingly Luso-Iberian in its European roots, is not exclusively so. During the past quarter century a significant number of former British colonies have gained independence and have thus added to the region's heterogeneity. This evolution has often involved international tension, sometimes to the point of threatened armed conflict. Perhaps the best example of this phenomenon is that involving the small Central American nation of Belize, formerly British Honduras. There the process of independence was delayed and complicated by Guatemala's persistent claims to the area. With fewer than 150,000 inhabitants, Belize could not emerge from under Great Britain's protective shield until a viable agreement could be reached with its much larger neighbor.

In cultural and social terms, this infant nation is essentially a displaced piece of the Caribbean—part of Central America in only a geographic sense. To a large extent this individuality is evident in Belize's politics as well. These considerations add to, rather than detract from, Belize's value to comparative study. Moreover, a full-scale book is particularly timely at this juncture since this very young nation has recently undergone its first really significant political shift when long-time leader George Price was overwhelmingly voted out of power at the end of 1984. Because of a prevalent tendency throughout world media to identify Belize with Price, this development may be a possible foretaste of increased political volatility in one of the globe's most conflict-ridden areas, a region of political as well as geological volcanoes.

Fortunately, a highly qualified scholar was available to undertake the task of profiling this little-known country. Professor O. Nigel Bolland is intimately familiar with contemporary Belize and has deeply and sensitively probed its past to explain its origins and development. With Mexico, Guatemala, and Honduras already analyzed in this series— as well as less immediate neighbors like Cuba, the Dominican Republic, and Nicaragua—this concise and balanced survey of Belize both completes the coverage of an important arc of Latin America and inaugurates the treatment of its non-Hispanic components. Thus, it makes a truly significant contribution to *Nations of Contemporary Latin America*.

Ronald M. Schneider

Acknowledgments

People in academic professions have many and various debts. During my many years of studying Belize, most of my debts have been intellectual and social, and I wish to acknowledge some of them here.

I first visited Belize in 1968. Before then, I owed much of my intellectual development to some fine teachers, including Peter Worsley and Ivar Oxaal at the University of Hull. Since then, I have been influenced by the example and stimulation of Ken Post, Arnie Sio, and Grant Jones, among many others. From the example of their scholarship, and their interest and understanding of the processes of colonization and decolonization, of slavery and of populist movements, I have learned a great deal. It is not their fault if I have not reached their high level, but they are largely responsible for establishing the standards I try to achieve, and for that I thank them.

Since 1968, I am fortunate to have had good institutional support, first from the Institute of Social and Economic Research of the University of the West Indies and later from Colgate University. I gratefully acknowledge this support and thank in particular the Research Council of Colgate University for financing my visit to Belize in January 1984 and for paying for the preparation of this manuscript.

My debts to Belizeans are incalculable. So many people have helped me for so many years that they must, please, forgive me for not thanking them all individually. However, I do wish to thank especially the helpful staff of the National Archives and, most of all, my friends Jo and Assad Shoman and Joan and Said Musa for their warm hospitality and encouragement.

I want to thank Melanie Goldstein for her cheerful and efficient work in typing this manuscript, Ellen Peletz for professionally drawing the map, and Pat Peterson for helpful editing. I also thank the Johns Hopkins University Press for permission to use materials from my earlier book on Belize, *The Formation of a Colonial Society* (Baltimore, 1977), and the Belize Government Information Service for the photographs.

Finally, I thank my family—Ellie, Kate, and Monica—for their love and help over many years, but especially during the difficult summer when I wrote this book. One of their rewards, I hope, will be more trips to the Belize we love.

O. Nigel Bolland

Author's Note

Unless stated otherwise, the dollars referred to in the text are Belizean dollars, which have been worth US$0.50 since 1976.

In the notes, *BA* refers to Belize Archives, Belmopan, and *CO* refers to Colonial Office records, Public Records Office, London.

BELIZE

1

Introduction: The Land

A map of Belize indicates the progressive humanization of the Belizean terrain. The ruined temples of the ancient Maya, as well as the roads, farms, and towns of the present, reveal a history of humans laboring to transform a natural wilderness into a habitable country: Forests have been cleared, fields created, drainage ditches dug, houses and roads built. The map is an enlightening document, but the landscape itself is a rich historical record for those who are prepared to read it. For generations innumerable persons have used their hands, arms, and backs to cut trees, move stones, build walls, and plant crops in a centuries-old relationship between the people and their environment. The various peoples who have come to this corner of the world have brought skills and traditions with them and, in the course of living in Belize, have evolved new customs, relationships, and institutions that are distinctively Belizean. The interaction of the people with their environment is therefore a fundamental aspect of the history of Belize, and its study is crucial to understanding its contemporary culture, economy, and society.

Although located within the northern tropics (between 15° 54′ and 18° 29′ north latitude), Belize's climate is subtropical, with average temperatures ranging from 24°C (75°F) in January to 27°C (81°F) in July. The country may be said to consist of three geographical regions. First, the northern low-lying plain, which is frequently swampy and linked by innumerable rivers, creeks, and lagoons, extends from the western low plateau to the Caribbean Sea. Second, in the south, the Maya Mountains run northeast and southwest, rising to Victoria Peak (3,680 feet), between the high plateau

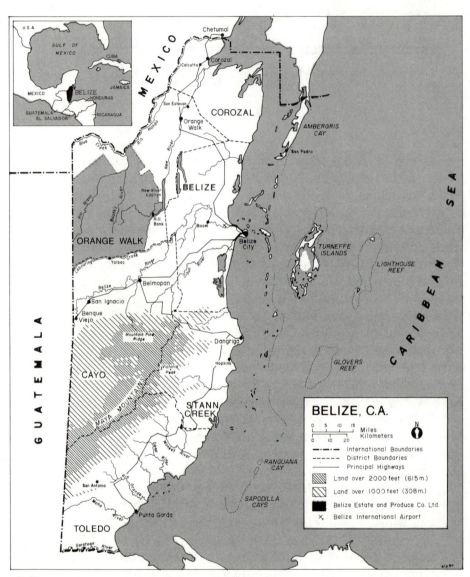

Belize

of Mountain Pine Ridge and the narrow coastal strip. The third region consists of the coastal waters dotted with cayes that contain a barrier reef between ten and twenty miles offshore, and the Turneffe Islands, lying forty-five miles east of Belize City. Together, these three regions, bounded by Mexico in the north and Guatemala in the west and south, include some 8,866 square miles of land (about 23,000 square kilometers), an area slightly larger than El Salvador and about twice the size of Jamaica.

Belize, which is only about 174 miles long and 68 miles broad at its widest point if we do not include the cayes, is characterized by a variety of geological formations, landscapes, and even climates. The northern plain consists of a limestone plateau having a potentially fertile soil and experiencing an annual rainfall of forty to sixty inches. The Maya Mountains, consisting of slates and granites, are hard and ancient, and rainfall in the south averages between 100 and 160 inches per year. The coastal waters are shallow and studded with coral reefs and sandy cayes that shift when struck by hurricanes. Although the climate is normally hospitable, the seasonal hurricane threat is serious because several coastal towns, including Belize City, Corozal, and Punta Gorda, have been devastated by winds of 100 miles per hour and high waves since 1931. Generally, however, an annual mean temperature of 79°F and humidity of 83 percent, mitigated by sea breezes, make a comfortable subtropical climate.

A notable geographical feature of Belize, which has for long played an important part in its development, is the river system. From the years of trade and riverine settlement of the ancient Maya to the transport of giant mahogany trees to the coast for export, the rivers, creeks, and lagoons have constituted the major network of communication. The northern plain is drained primarily by the Rio Hondo, Belize's northern boundary, and the New, Belize, and Sibun Rivers and their many tributaries. In the south, the rivers coming from the Maya Mountains, including the Monkey, Deep, Grande, Moho, and Sarstoon Rivers, the last of which is the southern boundary, are shorter and faster flowing. Few are navigable for any distance. Partly for this reason the northern part of Belize has been more developed and is more heavily settled. In the south, apart from the coastal settlements only a few villages are present, inhabited by Kekchi Maya who are engaged mostly in subsistence farming.

The climate, as well as the topography, has been important in the country's social and economic history. Great variations in rainfall have discouraged agriculture because crops frequently suffer from drought or flooding. Rainfall varies not only between regions but also from year to year at a single site; Punta Gorda, for example, may get less than 100 inches one year and more than 200 inches another year. The seasonal nature of the rainfall also influenced the seasonal cycle of work in the forestry industry: The dry season (January to April) is used for felling and trucking the trees to the river banks, and the following rainy season (May to October) is used for floating them on the swollen rivers to the sea. Today the seasonal variations in rainfall still affect people's livelihoods not only because of the agricultural cycle but also because the paucity of all-weather roads makes countrywide communications poor in the wet season.

Historically, the most important of Belize's natural resources has been the forests. The ancient Maya cleared the forests for agriculture and for ceremonial sites with stone axes and fire, as they lacked metal tools. Given such a dense forest environment, their cultural achievements are especially striking. When Europeans arrived on the Belizean coast in the sixteenth and seventeenth centuries they encountered chiefly humid, insect-infested mangrove swamps and found little land suitable for agriculture. Consequently, the great sugar revolution that transformed the Caribbean colonies from the middle of the seventeenth century did not take place in Belize. Instead, the British settlers extracted the logwood trees that were part of the scrubby vegetation near the coast and shipped them to their mother country for use in the woolen industry. By the 1770s the British were more interested in extracting mahogany for constructing furniture and ships, and later for building railway carriages. Mahogany trees, unlike logwood, grow scattered about in the mixed hardwood forests of the interior. The sparse plantation of the giant trees and the simple technology available for their extraction made only selective felling possible. The absence of any intensive forest exploitation meant that the "frontier" of the colony consisted of a number of temporary logging camps in an unsettled area. For years the colony resembled a vast timber reserve, linked to the metropolis by a primary town that was the chief population center and the location of the import and export trade.

Perhaps as much as 90 percent of the land is still covered by some kind of forest, though much of it is scrub pine of little commercial value. As the mahogany resources became depleted, other tropical hardwoods were extracted, including cedar, rosewood, and ziricote, as these have commercial value. In the south, mahogany was even more scarce, and the rivers less navigable, so most of the timber industry has been located in the northwest. As most of the land is occupied by rain forest, pine forest, or mangrove swamp, little is cultivated; between 12 and 15 percent of the 2.2 million acres suitable for agriculture are estimated to be actually farmed. Sugarcane is successfully grown on a large scale in the northern plain, and citrus fruits and bananas are grown in the southern valleys. In addition, production of rice, beans, and vegetables is expanding where soils are appropriate and markets accessible. Dairy and cattle industries, as well as those for poultry and apiculture, have recently begun, and a thriving fishing industry takes advantage of the coastal resources.

Apart from the cleared ceremonial centers of the Maya, the scattered ravages of the forest industry, and a handful of settlements—most of which are very small—the Belizean landscape was little affected by its human inhabitants until the last fifty years. Largely in this past half century have the roads been built, the fields permanently cleared, and new villages established. Construction of roads to link the major towns was begun in the 1930s, but large parts of the country are still remote from road transport or are serviced only by poor fair-weather tracks. The construction of the new capital, Belmopan, in 1970, symbolizes the intention to develop the interior. Though Belize City remains the dominant commercial and population center, the new country less and less resembles a trading port attached to a huge timber reserve. For many years Belize will continue to suffer from a colonial heritage that focused on the exploitation of its lands, people, and resources for metropolitan markets. Henceforth, it is hoped that the progressive development of the land, now proceeding apace, will be guided primarily by the needs of the Belizean people.

2

History from the Ancient Maya to the 1930s

As a nation, Belize is a product of the European colonization of the Americas in the sixteenth and seventeenth centuries. But long before the British settled in the Bay of Honduras and Columbus stumbled across the so-called New World, people had inhabited Central America, including the area now known as Belize.

The first people of the Americas came from Asia, when the Bering Straits was a frozen land bridge. As these people wandered south, following herds of animals, they adapted to different environments, and, 20,000 years ago, many cultures were present in North, Central, and South America. Before the Europeans arrived possibly 25 million people lived in Central America, but this population declined by as much as 90 percent in the first century of contact and conquest. By 1600, the indigenous peoples of the Caribbean were virtually extinct, and only about 1 million people remained in Central America. This demographic catastrophe—perhaps the largest in human history—resulted largely from the warfare and the social disruption caused by the conquest and the epidemics of European-borne diseases to which the indigenous people had no immunities.

Though the Belize that we know today is the result of colonization, the presence of the descendants of the ancient Maya and of many ruins of their great civilization warrants a brief summary of the precolonial history.

THE ANCIENT MAYA

It is hard to say just when or where the Maya emerged as a distinctive cultural group from the ancient peoples of Central America. Before 7000 B.C., the hunting and foraging bands of the region were generally small and very mobile; thus they left few remains other than stone tools at kill or camp sites. In the period before 2500 B.C., these seminomadic bands made the complicated transition to village farming. During the last thousand years of this archaic period most of the basic crops of later Mesoamerica, including maize, beans, squashes, and chile peppers, had been domesticated, but foraging and hunting continued to play a major part in the subsistence system. Around 5000 B.C., all the peoples living in Mesoamerica spoke related language dialects; the profusion of languages and cultures that subsequently characterized the region is associated with the later, more sedentary existence. The Maya speakers populated the area along the Gulf coast of Honduras, the lowland forests of Belize, Guatemala, and southern Mexico, and the highlands of Guatemala, but the great centers of Maya civilization flourished in the lowlands in the first millennium of the Christian era.

The peak of Maya civilization, known as the classic period, occurred between about A.D. 250 and A.D. 900–1000. The preclassic period from about 2500 B.C. to A.D. 250 is a fairly arbitrary construct, beginning with the appearance of the earliest known pottery and ending with the emergence of the basic institutions of Maya civilization. Belize boasts important sites of the earliest Maya settlements and late postclassic ceremonial construction, as well as majestic ruins of the classic period. At Cuello, about three miles west of Orange Walk, is the site of the earliest known Maya settlement, perhaps as early as 2500 B.C. Pottery—jars, bowls, and low-sided dishes—made by the villagers is the earliest found in Mesoamerica, and the platforms of buildings arranged around a small plaza indicate a distinctly Maya community. The presence of shell, hematite, and jade shows that the Maya were trading over long distances as early as 1500 B.C., though their economy was still basically subsistence, combining foraging and cultivation, hunting and fishing.

Cerros, a site on Corozal Bay, was a flourishing trade and ceremonial center between about 300 B.C. and A.D. 100. The temple platform is decorated with impressive seven-foot-high masks, representing the serpant god on either side of the central stairway. These are some distinguishing features of Maya civilization at an early date in northern Belize. The civic-ceremonial architecture of Maya civilization consisted of temples and palatial residences organized in groups around plazas built of cut stone, covered with stucco, and elaborately decorated and painted. The stylized carvings and paintings of people, animals, and gods and the geometric patterns on the buildings and sculptured steles constitute a highly developed art style. The Maya were also skilled at pottery making, jade carving, and flint knapping and made elaborate costumes of feathers. One of the finest carved jade objects of Maya civilization, the head of the sun god Kinich Ahau, was found in a tomb at Altun Ha, thirty-five miles north of Belize City.

Maya civilization was supported by farmers engaged in various types of agriculture, including labor-intensive irrigated and ridged field systems as well as shifting slash-and-burn agriculture. Their products fed the craft specialists, merchants, and warriors, as well as the priest-astronomers who coordinated the agricultural and other seasonal activities with a cycle of ceremonies. The latter group observed the movements of the sun, moon, and planets and developed a complex mathematical and calendrical system to coordinate various cycles of time and to record specific events on the carved steles.

In the late classic period probably at least 400,000 people inhabited the Belize area. Almost every part of the country worth cultivating was settled, as well as the cayes and coastal swamps. Caves in the mountains and limestone areas were used for shelter and for religious rituals, and hunters' tools have been found in the savanna and pine ridge areas. Most notable, however, and increasingly visited today by tourists are the many ceremonial centers, such as Altun Ha, already

Temple of the Masonry Altars, Altun Ha

mentioned, Xunantunich near Benque Viejo in the west, Nim Li Punit and Lubaantun in Toledo District, and Lamanai on the New River Lagoon. Xunantunich may have been occupied as early as 300 B.C., but most of the architecture in this partially excavated and breathtakingly beautiful site is of late classic construction. As in all the lowland Maya centers, the people who built Xunantunich continually constructed new temples and residences over older buildings, enlarging the platforms and raising the structures in the process. The great pyramid at Xunantunich, called El Castillo, rises 127 feet above the plaza floor and remains the highest manmade structure in Belize, offering an exciting view of the Mopan River and its surroundings.

In the tenth century Maya society suffered a severe breakdown from still unspecified causes, and the great civilization declined. Public building activity ceased, the administrative centers lost power, and the population declined as social and economic systems lost their coherence. At sites like Altun Ha and Xunantunich, some datable rubbish shows that people occupied the buildings as late as the thirteenth and fourteenth centuries, but they were no longer the splendid ceremonial and civic centers they once were. Recent scholarship suggests that "the decline involved complex processes in which external pressures exacerbated stresses inherent in the structure of Maya societies. Different combinations of factors resulted in slightly different processes and timings in each region."[1] The site of Lamanai dates from A.D. 150 to the late postclassic period. Even after the great centers of the Peten had been abandoned, the Maya of Lamanai continued refacing their ceremonial buildings. In fact, a substantial number of Maya were still living in the area when Franciscan friars built a church there, called Indian Church by the British, around the 1570s. The attempt to convert the Maya failed, but even after the Maya burned the church in 1641, they continued to live there. The Maya settlement at Lamanai spans many centuries, therefore, from the preclassic to the postcolonial periods.

The excavation of sites such as those at Cuello, Cerros, Altun Ha, and Lamanai has shown the extraordinary persistance of the Maya presence in Belize. Increasing information helps us understand the nature of Maya culture and society, their growth, achievements, and the decline of their ancient civilization, and suggests more continuities in their history than were hitherto thought possible. Contrary to the claims of colonially oriented historians, many Maya were still present in Belize when the Europeans came in the sixteenth and seventeenth centuries.

SPANISH AND BRITISH COLONIALISM

After the Papal Donation of 1493, Spain tried to maintain a monopoly in the Caribbean and Central America, leaving Brazil to Portugal. Northern European powers were increasingly attracted by the possibilities of trade and settlement in the New World. They resorted to smuggling, piracy, and war in the sixteenth and seventeenth centuries to challenge and then destroy Spain's monopoly. Early in the seventeenth century, the Dutch, British, and French encroached in the areas where Spain was weak—in the small islands of the eastern Caribbean and the no man's land of the Guianas between the Spanish and Portuguese dominions. Later in the seventeenth century, the British effectively challenged Spain in the western Caribbean, capturing Jamaica in 1655 and settling in the Bay of Honduras at about the same time.

The Spanish had been active in the Belize area for more than a century before the arrival of the British, but they never settled in Belize. Columbus was blown into the Gulf of Honduras during his fourth voyage in 1502, and a few years later Pinzón and Solis sailed northward along the coast of Belize to Yucatán. In 1519 the history of the region was transformed by Cortez's expedition to Mexico. After Cortez conquered the Aztec empire he sent expeditions to Guatemala and Honduras, and the conquest of Yucatán was undertaken in 1527. When Cortez himself passed through the southwestern corner of Belize in 1525, scattered settlements of Manche Chol Maya were in that area. These were later forcibly removed by the Spanish to the Guatemalan highlands when they "pacified" the region in the seventeenth century. The chief Spanish incursions into Belize came from Yucatán, however, and encountered stiff resistance from the Maya province of Chetumal, the capital of which was located near Corozal Town. It has been suggested that the Belize area became a place of refuge from the Spanish onslaught; however, if that was the case, the escaping Maya brought with them diseases contracted from the Spanish, resulting in a decimation of the population and a weakening of its resistance.

In the seventeenth century Spanish missionaries from Merida traveled up the New River and established churches in Maya settlements with the intention of converting the people. In 1618 they built a church at Tipu, a Maya town of about five hundred people, recently rediscovered near Negroman in the Cayo District. The Maya of Tipu, like those of Lamanai, burned the church and resisted the Spanish. In 1695 the Spanish again attempted to establish a mission at Tipu, but news of disturbances among the nearby Itza of Tayasal led them to retreat and we do not hear of Tipu again. By that time, British pirates and logwood cutters were already settling in the swampy coastline, and the eighteenth century witnessed a sporadic but prolonged rivalry between these two colonial powers for this piece of Central America.

British settlements on Old Providence and Ruatan off the coasts of Nicaragua and Honduras, respectively, were expelled by the Spanish in 1641 and 1642. At about that time British buccaneers, possibly including some refugees from the other settlements, used the tricky coastline of Belize as a base from which to attack Spanish ships. Although the origins of the British settlement in Belize are still obscure, some of the buccaneers appear to have changed from plundering Spanish logwood ships to cutting the wood themselves in various parts of the Yucatán peninsula in the 1650s and 1660s. The dye obtained from logwood—much in demand in the European woolen industry—was the chief raison d'etre of British settlement in the Bay of Honduras for at least a century. The shift from buccaneering to logwood cutting and more permanent settlement was encouraged by the 1670 Treaty of Madrid, in which the great powers agreed to suppress piracy. Conflict continued between Britain and Spain, however, over the right to cut logwood and to settle in Belize. During the eighteenth century, the Spanish attacked the British settlers repeatedly and on four occasions, in 1717, 1730, 1754, and 1779, forced them to leave. The Spanish never settled in Belize, however, and the British always returned to expand their trade and settlement.

At the end of the Seven Years' War in 1763, the Treaty of Paris conceded to the British the right to cut and export logwood but asserted Spanish sovereignty over the territory. When a new treaty was signed at Versailles in 1783 the terms were similar: The British were allowed to cut only logwood in a limited area between the Hondo and Belize Rivers. The logwood trade had declined by then, and mahogany had become the chief export so the settlers petitioned for a new agreement. By the Convention of London, signed in 1786, the Baymen, as they were called, were allowed to cut logwood and mahogany as far south as the Sibun River, but they could not build forts, establish any form of government, or develop agriculture. Spain retained sovereignty over the area and asserted the right to inspect the settlement twice a year. In 1798 a Spanish attack was beaten off at St. George's Cay, and this was Spain's last attempt to control the territory or to dislodge the British. Britain was slow to assert its own claim to sovereignty, but Spain soon lost its mainland colonies and British possession of Belize remained stable and unchallenged. Though Britain ceased to recognize Spanish sovereignty by the mid-nineteenth century, its formal claims were ambiguous until British Honduras was declared a colony in 1862. Because of these ambiguities Guatemala has claimed rights over Belize on the grounds that it inherited the sovereign rights of Spain. As will be seen in Chapter 5, the sovereignty of Belize is still disputed by Guatemala.

As the British consolidated their settlement and pushed deeper into the interior in search of mahogany in the late eighteenth century, they encountered resistance from the Maya. In 1788, for example, a Maya attack on a mahogany camp up New River was reported, and in 1802 troops were requested to "be sent up river to punish the Indians who are committing depredations upon the Mahogany works."[2] The Maya continued to fight back, and "vast hordes of Indians" reportedly attacked the mahogany camps as late as 1817.[3]

Of course, the British, not the Maya, were "committing depredations" and engaging in plunder as they made the Maya refugees in their own land. It is impossible to estimate how many Maya lived within the bounds of present-day Belize early in the nineteenth century, but those historians who asserted that they had abandoned the area before the seventeenth century are transparent colonial apologists.[4] Far from the British having peaceably colonized an uninhabited area, as these historians have claimed, they forcibly dispossessed and colonized the indigenous Maya. The British viewed the slash-and-burn agriculture of the Maya as a threat to their timber reserve, and, because they could not control and organize the Maya as a labor force, they sought to replace them with an imported population of African slaves.

SLAVERY AND ITS ABOLITION

Slavery in Belize, unlike slavery in most of the Americas, was not associated with the production of plantation crops like cotton and sugar. In Belize, slavery was organized for the extraction of timber, first logwood and then mahogany. This fact provokes the question about whether this difference in economic function gave rise to significant variations in the organization, conditions, and treatment of slaves. Recent findings have illuminated this question and refuted the old claims that slavery in Belize was "much less oppressive than elsewhere."[5]

The earliest reference to black slaves in the British settlement at Belize is in a 1724 Spanish missionary's account where it is stated that they were imported a short time before from Jamaica and Bermuda. A century later, an estimated 1,500 Africans were present in a slave population of about 2,300, "the remainder being Creoles and descendants of Indians,"[6] the latter brought from the Mosquito Shore in 1787. Whether the slaves were brought directly from Africa or through West Indian slave markets, the majority were African born, probably from the Bight of Benin and the Congo and Angola, as these were the principal sources of British slaves in the late eighteenth century. The Eboes or Ibos seem to have been particularly numerous; one section of Belize Town was known as Eboe Town in the first half of the nineteenth century. At least until the mid-nineteenth century, many of the African tribal identifications and cultural practices and distinctions appear to have persisted, even while the process of creolization was creating a new, more homogeneous Afro-Belizean culture.

By the mid-eighteenth century, the slaves made up the majority of the Belize population and by the turn of the century constituted about three-fourths of the population, the remainder consisting of whites (10 percent) and "free people of colour" (14 percent). Shortly before emancipation in 1838 slaves composed less than half the population, whereas the free blacks and colored had increased to about one-half and whites remained about one-tenth of the population. Although whites were a tiny minority in the settlement, they monopolized the power and wealth by dominating the chief economic activities of timber cutting and trade and by controlling the primitive legislative, judicial, and administrative institutions. As a result, the British settlers had a disproportionate influence on the development of the creole culture, for example, through the work of Anglican, Baptist, and Methodist missionaries. However, chiefly through their domination of the political and economic system they repressed the African cultural heritage.

Woodcutting was seasonal, requiring workers to spend several months isolated in temporary makeshift camps in the forest, away from their families in Belize Town. Logwood, a small tree that grows in clumps near the coast, could be cut by the settlers with just one or two slaves, but as the trade shifted to mahogany in the last quarter of the eighteenth century, the British settlers needed more money, land, and slaves for larger-scale operations. After 1770 about 80 percent of all male slaves aged ten years or more were woodcutters. The trees were found by huntsmen, then cut, trimmed, and trucked to the riverside. During the rainy season rafts of logs were floated down river to be squared at the mouth for shipment. The huntsmen were highly skilled and valued slaves, as were the axemen who cut the trees while standing on a springy platform twelve to fifteen feet high. Cattlemen cared for the cattle that pulled the huge logs to the river, and other members of the gang trimmed the trees and cleared the tracks. It was said that "The gangs of negroes employed in this work consist of from ten to fifty each; few exceed the latter number. The large bodies are commonly divided into several small ones, a plan which it is supposed greatly facilitates labour."[7] Here, then, is one difference in the work experience of Belizean slaves and those who worked in large gangs on the plantations elsewhere. The smaller gangs of woodcutters reduced the need for close supervision, and the whip-wielding drivers, who were ubiquitous on the plantations, were unknown in Belize.

As elsewhere, the masters in Belize had a small army of domestic slaves, mostly women and children, who cleaned their houses, sewed, washed, and ironed their clothes, cooked and served their food, and raised their children. Some of the slaves cultivated provisions—known in Belize as "making plantations"—to save the masters some of the cost of importing food or sometimes to sell or consume themselves. Other occupations among the slaves included sailor, blacksmith, nurse, and baker, but few slaves could hope to work in a skilled or pleasant job. Young people started work by waiting on their masters' tables, where they were taught to obey; then most of the young women continued in domestic work whereas the young men became woodcutters. As they became older or sick, men were transferred to the provision grounds. The rigid division of labor and the narrow range of work experience of most slaves limited their opportunities after legal emancipation in 1838.

The work experience of slaves in Belize, though different from that on plantations, was nevertheless oppressive. They were frequently the objects of "extreme inhumanity,"[8] as Superintendent Arthur stated in 1820. The settlement's chaplain reported "instances, many instances, of horrible barbarity"[9] against the slaves. The slaves' own actions, including suicide, abortion, murder, escape, and revolt, suggest how they viewed slavery. Slaves living in small, scattered, and remote groups could relatively easily escape in Belize if they were willing to leave their families. In the eighteenth century many escaped to Yucatán, and in the early nineteenth century a steady flow of runaways went to Guatemala or down the coast to Honduras. Some runaways established maroon communities within Belize, such as one near the Sibun River—"very difficult to discover and guarded by poisonous stakes"[10]—that offered refuge for other runaways. When freedom could be attained by slipping into the bush, revolt was not such a pressing option. Nevertheless, four revolts are recorded, in 1765, 1768, 1773, and 1820. The last, led by two black slaves, Will and Sharper, involved a considerable number of well-armed slaves. The superintendent stated that the slaves "had been treated with very unnecessary harshness by their Owner, and had certainly good grounds for complaint."[11]

One way the settler minority maintained its control was by dividing the slaves from the growing population of free blacks and colored who were given just enough privileges to make them petition for more. Though they were legally free, they could not hold commissions in the military nor act as jurors or magistrates, and their economic activities were restricted. To vote in elections they had to own more property and have lived in the area longer than the whites. These "favors," however, seemed sufficient to gain their allegiance as they frequently stressed their loyalty and European culture and tried to maintain their distinctiveness from black African slaves. When the free colored in other West Indian colonies were being given equal rights with whites, the Colonial Office threatened to dissolve the Baymen's legislative assembly, the Public Meeting, unless it followed suit. On 5 July 1831, the "coloured Subjects of Free Condition" were granted civil rights in Belize, a few years before the abolition of slavery.

By the time of legal emancipation in 1838, the essential nature of Belize, as a rigidly hierarchical and authoritarian colonial society in which people were ranked according to race and class in a structure of great inequalities, was well established. The act to abolish slavery throughout the British colonies was passed in June 1833 and did not produce drastic changes, nor was it meant to. The act included two generous measures for slave owners: a system of apprenticeship calculated to extend their control over the former slaves who were to continue to work for the same masters without pay, and compensation for the former slave owners for their loss of property. These measures helped to ensure that, even when the slaves were legally freed after apprenticeship was abolished in 1838, the majority of the population would be poor and landless, dependent for work upon their former owners who still monopolized the land. Before 1838, the land of Belize was grabbed by a handful of the principal inhabitants, who also owned most of the people, but after 1838 Crown land was no longer to be freely granted for fear that allowing the exslaves to obtain land might "discourage labour for wages."[12] The masters of Belize continued to control their former slaves by denying them access to land, but, by the mid-nineteenth century, the settler elite was itself changing as a new form of colonial domination emerged.

THE RISE AND DECLINE OF THE SETTLER OLIGARCHY

By the end of the eighteenth century a few settlers, who called themselves the principal inhabitants, dominated the

economy. There was no Crown land as Britain then acknowl-
edged Spanish sovereignty, but by a series of resolutions
passed in 1787, known as location laws, the chief settlers
simply allocated land to themselves and treated it as freehold
private property. The shift from logwood to mahogany cutting
in the late eighteenth century encouraged the concentration
of landownership and the evolution of a settler oligarchy.
Within months of the location laws being passed, the superintendent reported that twelve of the Old Baymen held
four-fifths of the available land under the 1786 treaty, or
about 2,000 square miles. The other great concentration of
property was in slaves. In 1790, the twenty largest estates
possessed a total of 1,085 slaves, or about half of all slaves
in the settlement. These same men used their connections
with London merchants to develop the import trade—so vital
since the local cultivation of provisions was still prohibited—
and consequently controlled retailing. They fixed the price of
logwood and mahogany and determined taxation.

From this economic basis the wealthy cutters controlled
the political system of the settlement in the form of the Public
Meeting and the Magistracy. The settler oligarchy succeeded
in challenging the Crown's representative when it got Superintendent Despard suspended in 1789, and when Superintendent Arthur attacked what he called the "monopoly on
the part of the monied cutters" in 1817, he was only partially
successful. He proclaimed that all unclaimed land was henceforth Crown land, to be granted only by the Crown's representative, but the existing monopoly of landownership was
unchanged. Arthur complained that his office was inadequately
defined and lacked the necessary authority. The small size of
the free population encouraged the propensity of the wealthiest
and longest-established settlers to fulfill several powerful roles
simultaneously. For example, Marshall Bennett, one of the
chief landowners and merchants of Belize, was the biggest
slave proprietor (with 271 slaves in 1826), a magistrate for
twenty-two of the thirty years between 1798 and 1828, and
the senior judge of the Supreme Court, a colonel of the
militia, the president of Arthur's commission on land, and
frequently the chairman of the Public Meeting. The oligarchy
continued to make and execute the laws and to administer

the public business in their private interests, and until 1854 the constitutional anomalies of Belize, which was a colony in all but name, remained unresolved.

The settler oligarchy used its political power to maintain its economic monopoly by making the rest of the population, even those free people whom they did not own outright, dependent upon them. The monopolization of land was maintained: not to use the land (which, despite their possession of hundreds of slaves, they could not do) but to deny its use to others. So long as the mahogany trade flourished, supplemented in the 1820s by a lucrative entrepôt trade with Central America, these wealthy settlers remained dominant. The mahogany trade had its ups and downs, of course, but the greatest boom, between 1835 and 1847, helped produce the greatest depression. High demand resulted in the cutting of all easily accessible trees, even young trees, and a serious depletion of timber resources. As the cutters moved further into the interior in search of mahogany, the cost of production rose. After a peak of almost 14 million feet exported in 1846, exports of mahogany fell to about 5.5 million feet in 1859 and only 2.75 million feet in 1870, the lowest recorded annual figure since the beginning of the century. Although mahogany and logwood continued to account for over 80 percent of the total value of exports, the price of these goods was so low that the economy was in a state of permanent depression after the 1850s. One major result of this depression was the increasing consolidation of capital and the intensification of metropolitan ownership.

The British Honduras Company, registered in 1859, emerged as the predominant landowner of the colony. Originating in a partnership between one of the old settler families and a London merchant, and registered as a limited company under the new Joint Stock Companies Act, the firm expanded, often at the expense of others who were forced to sell their land. In 1875 this firm became the Belize Estate and Produce Company, a metropolitan-based business that owned about half of all the privately owned land in the colony and has been the chief single force in Belize's political economy for over a century.

The concentration and centralization of capital in the hands of metropolitan companies, and of one in particular, have meant that the pattern of land use and the direction of the colony's economy have been largely determined in the companies' boardrooms. But it has also meant the almost complete eclipse of the settler elite as a major class within the colony's social structure. By 1881, only 375 of the 27,452 people in Belize, a little over 1 percent, were white, and of these 271 were males, indicating that few white families settled in Belize. That most of the whites were transient males is confirmed by the remark made in 1883 that "white people but look upon it as a resting, not an abiding place, one from which they hope eventually to return enriched to their native soil."[13] The settlers were further eclipsed when they lost control of the chief political and administrative institutions.

In the late 1820s the white settlers faced a serious political predicament. Threatened by the growing demands of the free colored group, the oligarchy accepted a partial curtailment of its political privileges when in 1832 the superintendent took the authority to appoint the magistrates, hitherto the keystone of the settlers' political-administrative system. When the British government insisted on extending civil rights to the free colored, abolishing slavery in Belize and appointing special magistrates to oversee the apprenticeship period, it was asserting British control over the territory, though it was not yet formally a colony. The Public Meeting, significantly, was losing power at the same time that it was including a higher proportion of colored members. Any British-born resident with property worth £300 could be elected for life provided twenty-five registered voters voted for him, but he would lose his voting rights if he suffered a loss of property. By 1848, the superintendent reported that only thirty-three of the sixty-four members were qualified to vote. Hence, "the real governing body consists of 5 or 6 Mahogany Houses in Belize whose operations are almost entirely dependent on certain other Houses in London."[14] The care with which the oligarchy had protected itself against the free colored, by instituting a restrictive and self-perpetuating membership, had resulted by midcentury in the shift of the real locus of decision-making from the Public Meeting to the metropolitan companies.

Along with these changes in the political economy of Belize, a number of broader international factors combined in the midcentury to amend the settlement's anomolous constitutional status. Neither when Spain recognized Mexican independence in 1836 nor when Britain recognized the independence of Guatemala in 1849 was any reference made to the British settlement in Belize. In the Clayton-Bulwer Treaty of 1850 Britain and the United States agreed to promote the construction of a canal and to refrain from colonizing any part of Central America. Although the British government interpreted the latter as applying only to any future occupation, the U.S. government, particularly after 1853 when an aggressively expansionist administration emphasized the Monroe Doctrine, claimed that Britain was obliged to evacuate the area. Britain yielded on the Bay Islands and the Mosquito Shore but in 1854 produced a formal constitution for its possession of Belize. The exigencies of international diplomacy coincided with the agitations of the superintendent to produce these constitutional changes.

The Legislative Assembly of 1854 was to have a four-year life and only eighteen elected members, each of whom had to have £400 worth of property, and three official members appointed by the superintendent. The restrictive-class nature of this legislature was reinforced by the fact that voters had to have property yielding an income of £7 a year or a salary of £100 a year. That the assembly could be prorogued or dissolved by the superintendent at any time and that he could originate legislation and give or withhold consent to bills—all suggested that the legislature was more a chamber of debate than of decision-making and that the Colonial Office was henceforth to be the real political-administrative power in Belize. In 1862 British Honduras was declared a colony and the Crown's representative was elevated to a lieutenant governor.

In 1871 further constitutional developments took place: The Legislative Assembly abolished itself after a life of only seventeen years, and the British government established its total control over the colony. As elsewhere in the British West Indies, the imperial government was imposing its more direct rule in a Crown colony system by abolishing the elected assemblies and governing through a wholly appointed Legislative Council. A crisis in Belize in the early 1870s was caused by the conflicts between the British and the Maya, who had been resisting British domination determinedly since 1866. During the Guerra de las Castas in Yucatán, a devastating war that halved the population of Yucatán between 1847 and 1855, many thousands of refugees—white, Maya, and Mestizo—fled south to Belize. Most of these refugees were small farmers, who by 1857 were said to be growing considerable quantities of sugar, rice, corn, and vegetables in the Northern District. Some of the Maya, who had risen against the Mexican authorities and had no wish to be subjects of the British, settled in the remote area of the Yalbac Hills, just beyond the woodcutters' frontier in the upper reaches of Booth's River and Labouring Creek. By 1862 about 1,000 Maya were established in ten villages, with the center in San Pedro.[15] One group of Maya, led by Marcos Canul, attacked a mahogany camp on the Rio Bravo in 1866 and demanded ransom for prisoners and rent for the land. A detachment of British troops sent to San Pedro was routed later that year. Early in 1867 over 300 troops marched into the Yalbac Hills and destroyed the Maya villages, provision grounds, and granaries in an attempt to drive them out of the district. In April 1870 Canul and his men marched into Corozal and occupied the town.

Largely as a result of the costly military expeditions against the Maya, the expenses of administering the colony had increased in the 1860s, at a time when the economy was severely depressed. The Legislative Assembly, which controlled the colony's revenues and expenditures, was dominated by great landowners and merchants. Though some of the landowners were also involved in commerce, their interest differed from the other merchants of Belize Town: The former resisted the taxation of land and favored an increase on import duties whereas the latter preferred the opposite. Moreover, the merchants of Belize Town felt relatively secure from Maya attacks and were unwilling to contribute toward the protection of mahogany camps, whereas the landowners felt that requiring them to pay taxes on lands given inadequate protection was unjust. These conflicting interests produced a stalemate in the assembly, which failed to authorize the raising of sufficient revenue. Unable to agree among themselves, the members of the assembly surrendered their political privileges in return for the greater security of a Crown colony, and the new constitution was inaugurated in April 1871. A year later, Canul attacked the barracks at Orange Walk with 150 men. After several hours of fighting they retired, and Canul, mortally wounded, died on 1 September 1872. That was the last serious attack on the colony, and the Maya were subsequently forced to give up their independent existence and live on reservations.

Under the new constitution, Belize was governed by the governor-in-council, the council consisting of five official and four unofficial members, all nominated. This constitutional change confirmed and completed a change in the locus and form of power in the colony's political economy that had been evolving during the preceding half century.

SOCIAL CHANGES IN A STAGNANT ECONOMY

Although the political and economic institutions of the colonizing group in Belize evolved in relation to the changing interests of the metropolis, they also were altered by changes in the nature of, and the relations within, the colonial social structure. Belize consists of a variety of racial and ethnic groups and social classes that participate unequally in the same economy and polity, but they do not subscribe to a common culture or ideology. What held these various groups and classes together, in fact, was the monopoly of power of the colonizers. Although this monopoly was consolidated in the last decades of the nineteenth century, significant changes were taking place in the social structure of Belize, changes that had important repercussions in the political process in the twentieth century. In fact, it may be said that the tension between the social changes, on one hand, and the stagnation in the political economy, on the other, were behind the labor disturbances and the early independence movement of the 1930s through 1950s.

Chief among the social changes of the nineteenth century was the influx of thousands of people, mostly refugees, who changed the social and cultural profile of Belize. Until the mid-nineteenth century, most of the population of the settlement was of African origin. In 1823, some three-fifths of the slaves, or about 37 percent of the total population, were African-born. Though the slave trade was abolished in 1807, 459 "liberated" Africans from Spanish slavers were landed in Belize in 1836. Many of these died of disease, suicide, or accidents soon after their arrival; only 357 remained at the end of 1837. Few people came from Africa after that, and by 1861 only 3.5 percent of the population was African-born. About the same proportion had been born in the British West Indies, mostly in Jamaica and Barbados, and it may be assumed that most of these were of African ancestry, joining the descendants of Africans in Belize to swell the Creole population.

Another group that came to Belize in the first half of the nineteenth century was the Garifuna, descendants of the Caribs of the eastern Caribbean and Africans who had escaped from slavery. The Garifuna resisted British and French colonialism in the Windward Islands until they were defeated by the British in 1796, and 5,000 of them were transported across the Caribbean to the Bay Islands in the Gulf of Honduras. From there they migrated to the Caribbean coasts of Nicaragua, Honduras, Guatemala, and southern Belize. By 1802, about 150 Garifuna had settled in the Stann Creek area; these engaged principally in fishing and growing ground foods. In 1811, as they were bringing produce to the market in Belize Town, the magistrates ordered them to get a permit from the superintendent or quit the settlement within forty-eight hours. Many Garifuna later came to Belize after a civil war in Honduras. They were soon employed alongside slaves as mahogany cutters. Judging from the fact that a constable was appointed in Stann Creek to apprehend "runaway Caribs," they, too, appear to have resisted coercion. In 1841, Dangriga, their largest settlement, was described as a flourishing village, and an American traveller described the Garifuna village of Punta Gorda as having 500 inhabitants and displaying a wide variety of fruits and vegetables.

Though they had productively used the land in the south for over fifty years, the Garifuna were treated by the British as squatters and were told in 1857 that they must obtain leases from the Crown or they might lose their lands and any buildings on them. Even though the white settlers, who had gratuitously allocated vast tracts of land to themselves, were given legal titles to such land under the Laws in Force Act of 1855, the Garifuna were discriminated against. Later, Governor Longden stated that small plantations, though occupied for over fifty years, could be sold "over the heads of the present occupiers to large proprietors,"[16] and the Crown Lands Ordinance of 1872 established Garifuna as well as Maya reservations. The Garifuna, like the Maya, were prevented from owning their own land independently and were treated as squatters and a source of valuable labor.

The largest number of immigrants to Belize in the nineteenth century were Maya and Mestizos who fled the Guerra de las Castas in Yucatán and settled in the north. By 1857, the town of Corozal, then six years old, had 4,500 inhabitants, second only to Belize Town with 7,000; San Estevan, with 1,300 Yucatecos, was the colony's third largest town. The 1861 census revealed that 9,817 persons, or 38 percent of the total population, had been born in Mexico. Another 2,565 persons living in Belize had been born in Honduras, Guatemala, and Nicaragua: Together, 85 percent of the foreign-born population of Belize in 1861 was from Latin American countries. Of the 25,635 people enumerated in Belize in that year, perhaps 10,000 were Spanish or Mestizo and 5,000 were Maya. By the mid-nineteenth century, then, the chief ethnic communities of Belize were established: the mostly English-speaking, Protestant, Creole people of African descent, centered in Belize Town; the mostly Spanish-speaking, Catholic, Maya and Mestizo people living chiefly in the north and west; and the Garifuna on the southern coast.

Other immigrants came from India and China. The British West Indian colonies imported about 548,000 indentured laborers from India between 1838 and 1917, most of them to Guyana and Trinidad. When some sugar estates were started in Corozal and Toledo Districts, a few hundred Indians were brought to Belize, and their descendants, now largely creolized, still live in communities such as Calcutta in Corozal District. Chinese laborers were less fortunate: Of 474 Chinese immigrants brought from Amoy in 1865 to work on the estates of the British Honduras Company on the New River, over 100 died and about 100 more fled to Mexico because of bad food, overwork, and cruel treatment by the estate manager. By 1868 only 211 were left, and Governor Longden referred in 1869 to a "small remnant" of 193 Chinese laborers working on the estates. According to the censuses, the number of Chinese immigrants was only 133 in 1871 and fell steadily thereafter; the number of Indian immigrants peaked at 291 in 1891. The visible Chinese minority in Belize today is composed of more recent immigrants who have come since the 1920s.

The last major group of immigrants to Belize in the nineteenth century were Maya, some from the Peten area of Guatemala into the Cayo District, and others from the Vera Paz area of Guatemala into Toledo District. The former are Mopan Maya who fled heavy taxes and forced labor and have become more integrated into the national life than the latter, Kekchi Maya, who have lived for a century in a cluster of isolated villages around San Antonio, Toledo. Although by no means segregated—roads and radios, Catholic churches and schools, all draw them into the national life—the Kekchi are among the most traditional and self-sufficient people in Belize today.

Although the population of Belize had its origins largely in immigration, most of this movement had ended by the end of the nineteenth century. (Though further immigrations have taken place in recent years, notably among Mennonites and Central American refugees, a net emigration has occurred from Belize in the twentieth century.) The 1861 census revealed that 57 percent of the population had not been born in Belize and that 85 percent of these foreign-born persons had come from the neighboring republics, chiefly Mexico. The number of Mexican-born residents declined after 1861, and the number from Honduras and Guatemala reached a peak about the turn of the century. Persons born in Africa and those from the British Caribbean each constituted about 6 percent of the foreign-born population in 1861, but as the former declined, the latter increased; hundreds of Jamaicans, in particular, came to Belize in the late nineteenth century. After 1861, the proportion of the population that was foreign born declined steadily—to 31 percent in 1881, 24 percent in 1901, 13 percent in 1931, and 8 percent in 1960. The assimilation of these diverse immigrants and their descendants into the colonial society has been one of the chief sources of social change in Belize.

Another important social change that occurred in the late nineteenth and early twentieth centuries was the rise of a Creole and Mestizo middle class, chiefly in the towns. Urbanization, itself an important process, is both a product and a source of social change in so far as it provides a new context for evolving social formations and institutions. The population of Belize City and the six next largest towns (Dangriga, Orange Walk, Corozal, San Ignacio, Punta Gorda, and Benque Viejo) tripled between 1881 and 1946, from 10,697 to 33,072, increasing as a proportion of the colony's population from 39 percent to 56 percent. Belize City, in particular, has shown a greater rate of increase than that of the whole population, from 5,767 persons in 1881 to 21,886 in 1946, an increase from 21 percent to 37 percent of the total population. The greatest annual rate of increase in Belize City, namely, 3 percent, took place in the 1920s, shortly before the Great Depression and a major hurricane shattered the town's economy and infrastructure.

Within these growing towns a slow but steady increase has occurred in the number and proportion of people in the middle classes, such as managers and lower government officials, professional service and clerical workers. The proportion of schoolteachers, male and female, in the gainfully occupied population, for example, increased from 0.3 percent in 1891 to 1.8 percent in 1946, a steady and significant increase of influential people. From among this small, relatively educated class of Creoles and Mestizos who, unlike the expatriate employees of the government and the metropolitan businesses, were committed to residence, properties, and careers in Belize, emerged some fairly articulate political demands of a liberal, incipient nationalism. Many members of the Creole elite continued to glorify all things British and to mimic what they imagined to be the gentleman's lifestyle of their mother country—as some still do today—but others resented the control of land, commerce, and government by a coterie of expatriates and developed a "Natives First" orientation. When they succeeded in co-opting support from the volatile working class, which had neither votes nor candidates of its own, these middle-class Belizeans were elected in 1936 to the first Legislative Council to include five elected members. Their success, limited to the role of a loyal opposition to the still-entrenched colonial government and metropolitan businesses, was based upon the rise of the urban middle classes and the agitation of the working classes. These phenomena themselves reflected important changes in the Belizean economy and its place in international capitalism.

The monopolization of land, the dominance of forestry interests and the suppression of agriculture, the prolonged depression in the mahogany trade, and the economic power of a nouveau riche merchant class, all contributed to the underdevelopment and stagnation that characterized the Belizean economy in the late nineteenth century. The Maya, Garifuna, and African peoples of Belize were denied secure titles to land and discouraged from farming pursuits. But when some of the Yucatecan immigrants succeeded with a more commercial agriculture in the 1850s, some of the big landowners, frustrated by the depression in the mahogany trade, started sugar estates. By 1868 over 3,000 acres were planted in cane, and 1,033 tons of sugar were produced, of which 762 tons were exported. The British Honduras Company, the largest landowner in Belize, was by far the biggest sugar producer, with four plantations and factories with steam machinery. Though various experiments were tried with other commercial crops, including coffee, cacao, cotton, bananas, coconuts, and cohune oil, by the end of the nineteenth century most of these efforts had failed. Sugar and rum production declined while Panama disease and rats destroyed most banana production. The failure of plantation agriculture left the Belizean economy dependent still upon forestry.

In the early twentieth century a brief revival in the forest industry took place as new demands for forest products came from the United States. Chicle, a gum taken from the sapodilla tree and used to make chewing gum, was an important prop to the economy from the 1880s. Much of the gum was tapped in the forests of Mexico and Guatemala, but the organization and labor for the industry were in Belize. Chicle was extracted during the rainy season from June to November, and many of the *chicleros* were Maya recruited by labor contractors. A short-lived boom in the mahogany trade occurred around 1900 in response to U.S. demand, but the ruthless exploitation of the forests without any conservation or reforestation had depleted resources. Not until the 1920s did the introduction of tractors revive the industry by opening up new areas, and the subsequent use of bulldozers, logging trucks, and all-weather roads extended the industry into the west and south. All this time mahogany remained the chief export and together with cedar and chicle made up 97 percent of forest production and 82 percent of the total value of exports.

Belize was still largely a logging camp, but by the early decades of this century its economy was increasingly dependent on the United States rather than on Britain. Much of the early direct U.S. investment in Belize was unsuccessful: A group of southerners started sugar estates in the Toledo District in 1867, but their settlement was practically over by 1910, and the United Fruit Company's 12,500-acre banana estate in Stann Creek Valley was abandoned not long after it was purchased in 1911. The chief economic influence of the United States in these decades was mainly through trade, and this commercial connection strengthened a new, indigenous mercantile elite in its competition with the old British firms.

The early British merchants of Belize had thrived on their monopoly of the import-export business, based upon their close connections with London merchants and their control of most people in Belize. The lucrative entrepôt trade with Central America encouraged the emergence of commercial houses that were independent of the mahogany companies, and, during the U.S. Civil War, some of these merchants benefited from contraband trade with the Confederates. With the decline of the mahogany trade, this merchant class extended its economic power in Belize, and, because it encouraged the preference for imported goods, it furthered the underdevelopment and dependency of the economy. By about 1890 most commerce in Belize was in the hands of a clique of Scottish and German merchants, most of whom were relative newcomers.

With the rise of trade with the United States, however, the traditional British political-economic connection was challenged by white and colored Creoles whose connections were with U.S. business. Such people as R. S. Turton, the Creole chicle buyer for Wrigley's of Chicago, and Henry I. Melhado, whose merchant family dealt in illicit liquor traffic during Prohibition, became major political as well as economic figures. By 1927, the representatives of the British landowners, who had dominated the Legislative Council since its inception, were largely replaced by Belize Creole merchants and professionals. The exception was the manager of the Belize Estate and Produce Company, who was an unofficial member of the council as a matter of course. The participation of this Creole elite in the political process, albeit as loyalists within a system of governance that excluded the elective principle entirely until 1936, was evidence of some of the emerging social changes largely concealed by economic stagnation. These changes accelerated with such force in the 1930s that they ushered in the new era of modern Belizean politics.

THE GREAT DEPRESSION
AND LABOR STRUGGLES OF THE 1930s

The Belizean economy was shattered by the Great Depression, and unemployment increased rapidly. The *Colonial Report for 1931* stated that "contracts for the purchase of mahogany and chicle, which form the mainstay of the Colony, practically ceased altogether, thereby throwing a large number of the woodcutters and chicle-gatherers out of work."[17] On top of this economic disaster, the worst hurricane in Belize's history demolished Belize City on 10 September 1931, killing over 1,000 people and destroying at least three-quarters of the housing. The British relief response was tardy and inadequate. While the British government seized the opportunity to impose Treasury control on the colony, endowing the governor with reserve powers, people in the city were making shelters out of the wreckage of their houses. The economy, meanwhile, continued to decline in 1932 and 1933: The total value of imports and exports in the latter year was $2,729,000, or little more than one-fourth of what it had been in 1929, namely, $9,934,000. This economic situation, aggravated by the disastrous hurricane, was responsible for severe hardship among the poor people of Belize. They responded in 1934 with a series of demonstrations, strikes, and riots that marked the beginning of modern politics and the independence movement of Belize.

Riots, strikes, and rebellions had occurred before in Belize's history—during the period of slavery and after—but the events of the 1930s were modern labor disturbances in the sense that they gave rise to organizations with articulate industrial and political goals and were not merely spontaneous protests. The riots of mahogany workers in 1894, provoked by a cut in their real wages caused by devaluation, and the riot of demobilized Creole servicemen in 1919 to protest racist treatment and the injustice of British domination were important phenomena and may have helped lay some basis for subsequent action, but they were soon stopped by British troops and had little lasting effect. In contrast, when a group calling itself the Unemployed Brigade marched through Belize City on 14 February 1934 to present demands to the governor, it started a broad movement. Out of desperation, the poor people of Belize turned to the governor, who responded by creating a little relief work, stone-breaking at $.10 a day, and offering a daily ration of a pound of badly cooked rice at the prison gates.

The unemployed, who demanded a cash dole, soon turned to Antonio Soberanis Gomez (1897–1975), a barber, who denounced the Unemployed Brigade's leaders at a meeting on 16 March 1934 and took over the movement. For the next few weeks, Soberanis and his colleagues of the Labourers and Unemployed Association (LUA) attacked the governor and his officials, the rich merchants, and the Belize Estate and Produce Company at biweekly meetings attended by 600 to 800 people. According to the police superintendent, "the more violent the language used from the rostrum the more the crowd enjoyed it."[18] When the workers made specific demands for relief and a minimum wage, these demands were couched in broad moral and political terms that began to define and develop a new nationalistic and democratic political culture. Before the end of 1934 Soberanis had organized a strike in Stann Creek and was arrested in connection with a major riot in Belize City. Under a new sedition law, Soberanis was jailed for a speech in Corozal in November 1935. Factionalism occurred within the LUA during his internment, and after his release in February 1936 the movement was less effective.

The labor agitation actually achieved a great deal. Of most immediate importance was the creation of relief work by a governor who saw it as a way to avoid civil disturbances. Over 200 miles of roads were built, using intensive labor on a rota system, every registered unemployed laborer being employed two weeks in every two months. Governor Alan Burns also pressed, against the wishes of the traditional landowning and merchant elite, for a semirepresentative government, and the newspapers, the *Clarion* and *Independent*, pressed for lower qualifications for the franchise than the unofficial members of the council recommended. When the new constitution was passed in April 1935, admitting the elective principle for the first time since 1871, it was with the high property and income qualifications demanded by the unofficial majority, who clearly had no interest in furthering democracy. This very limited change meant that members of the working class could not vote or be political candidates but could only encourage those more critical members of the

Creole middle classes in opposition to the big-business candidates. The Citizens' Political party and the LUA endorsed
Arthur Balderamos, a black lawyer, and R. S. Turton, a Creole
chicle millionaire, who became the chief opposition in the
new council of 1936. Working-class agitation continued, and
in 1939 all six elected seats on the Belize Town Board went
to middle-class Creoles who appeared more sympathetic to
labor. By that time several investigations and officials ac-
knowledged that Belizean workers had legitimate grievances,
and new labor legislation was advocated.

The greatest achievement of the working-class agitation
of the 1930s lay in the labor reforms passed between 1941
and 1943. Since emancipation, the workers of Belize had been
tightly controlled by labor contracts and by a combination
of advance and truck systems that induced indebtedness to
the employer. Investigators of labor conditions in the 1930s
were appalled to discover that workers received rations of
inferior flour and mess pork and tickets to be exchanged at
the commissaries, in lieu of cash wages. Workers and their
families suffered from malnutrition, and employers exploited
the system in a way reminiscent of slavery.[19] The law governing
labor contracts, the Masters and Servants Act of 1883, made
a breach of contract by the laborer a criminal offense, punishable by twenty-eight days imprisonment with hard labor.
In 1931 proposals to legalize trade unions and to introduce
a minimum wage and sickness insurance were all rejected
by Governor Burdon, but ten years later such legislation was
reconsidered. Trade unions were legalized in 1941, but rec-
ognition of unions by employers was not made compulsory,
and the penal clauses of the Masters and Servants Act rendered
the new rights ineffectual. Employers among the unofficial
members defeated a bill to repeal these penal clauses in
August 1941. The Employers and Workers Bill, passed on 27
April 1943, finally removed breach of labor contract from the
criminal code and enabled Belize's infant trade unions to
pursue the struggle for improving labor conditions. The General Workers Union, registered in 1943, quickly expanded into
a nationwide organization and provided crucial support for

Cutting a mahogany tree in the old way

the nationalist movement that took off with the formation of the People's United party in 1950.

The 1930s were a crucible of modern Belizean politics, a decade in which the old phenomena of exploitive labor conditions and authoritarian colonial and industrial relations began to give way to new industrial and political processes. The agitation produced by the economic and social crisis of the early 1930s stemmed from working-class discontent, and workers were able to win important reforms in the labor legislation by 1943. Politically, however, the very limited franchise of 1936, which enabled only 1.8 percent of the population to vote, ensured that political power, if it changed hands at all, would move only from the old appointed unofficial members of the council who represented British business interests to a new Creole business and professional elite who represented the rising middle class. The vast majority of Belizeans, workers whose political consciousness and activity were being spurred by desperation, had no vote, no candidates, and no party, but on the basis of their initiatives the independence movement grew.

NOTES

1. John S. Henderson, *The World of the Ancient Maya* (Ithaca, N.Y., Cornell University Press, 1981), p. 198.

2. Sir John Alder Burdon, ed., *Archives of British Honduras,* vol. 2 (London, Sifton Praed, 1935), p. 58.

3. Minutes from the public record, 25 February 1817, CO 123/26.

4. Burdon, *Archives*, vol. 1, p. 4. Stephen L. Caiger, *British Honduras: Past and Present* (London, Allen & Unwin, 1951), pp. 126–27; see O. Nigel Bolland, "The Maya and the Colonization of Belize in the Nineteenth Century," in *Anthropology and History in Yucatán*, Grant D. Jones, ed. (Austin, University of Texas Press, 1977), pp. 69–99.

5. D.A.G. Waddell, *British Honduras: A Historical and Contemporary Survey* (London, Oxford University Press, 1961), p. 14. See O. Nigel Bolland, "Slavery in Belize," *Journal of Belizean Affairs* 6 (1978):3–36, and *The Formation of A Colonial Society: Belize, from*

Conquest to Crown Colony (Baltimore, Johns Hopkins University Press, 1977), Chaps. 4–7.

6. Superintendent Codd to R. Wilmot, 23 February 1823, CO 123/34.

7. Captain George Henderson, *An Account of the British Settlement at Honduras* (London, 1809), p. 47.

8. Superintendent Arthur to Earl Bathurst, 7 October 1820, CO 123/29.

9. John Armstrong, *A Candid Examination of "The Defence of the Settlers of Honduras . . ."* (London, 1824), p. 61.

10. Burdon, *Archives*, vol. 2, p. 184; Arthur to Bathurst, 16 May 1820, CO 123/29.

11. Arthur to Bathurst, 16 May 1820, CO 123/33.

12. Lord Normanby to Superintendent Macdonald, 22 April 1839, BA, R 15.

13. Archibald Robertson Gibbs, *British Honduras: An Historical and Descriptive Account of the Colony from Its Settlement, 1670* (London, Sampson Low, 1883), p. 174.

14. Superintendent Fancourt to Earl Grey, 10 August 1848, CO 123/74.

15. See O. Nigel Bolland, "Maya Settlements in the Upper Belize River Valley and Yalbac Hills: An Ethnohistorical View," *Journal of Belizean Affairs* 3 (1974):3–23; Grant D. Jones, "Levels of Settlement Alliance among the San Pedro Maya of Western Belize and Eastern Peten, 1857–1936," in Jones, ed., *Anthropology and History in Yucatán*, pp. 139–189.

16. Governor Longden to Governor Grant, 6 March 1868, BA, R 98.

17. *The Colonial Report for 1931*, no. 1610 (London, His Majesty's Stationery Office, 1933), 13–14.

18. Minute paper 1666-34, 29 November 1934, BA, SP 25.

19. See O. Nigel Bolland, "Labour Conditions in Belize: The Century after 1838," *BELCAST Journal of Belizean Affairs* 1, no. 1 (1984):48–54.

3

The Peoples and Cultures

POPULATION

The most striking features of the population of Belize are its quantity and its cultural diversity. The small population, even more than the limited land area, distinguishes Belize from its neighbors. With about 155,000 people, Belize is the least populous sovereign nation on the American mainland (French Guiana has 73,000 people and some Caribbean islands have fewer people). Though the area of Belize is slightly larger than that of El Salvador and is about twice the size of Jamaica, the population density is only about seventeen persons per square mile.

The demographic history of Belize over the past 300 years may be conveniently divided into three periods. First, from the initial British settlement in the seventeenth century until 1845 the fluctuating population grew to about 10,000 persons. During the period of slavery, the slaves seem to have been unable to reproduce because of a high mortality rate caused by such factors as disease, malnutrition, ill treatment, overwork, and suicide, and because large numbers escaped from the settlement. When the slave trade was abolished in 1807, the population declined, but soon hundreds of Garifuna settled in Belize, and after emancipation in 1838 the population increased rapidly. The second period can be characterized as a century of sustained growth. The influx of thousands of refugees from Yucatán in the 1850s caused the population to double, and it reached almost 60,000 persons by the end of World War II. During the third period, about

TABLE 3.1
Total Population of Belize, 1861-1980

Date	Total Population
1861	25,635
1871	24,710
1881	27,452
1891	31,471
1901	37,479
1911	40,458
1921	45,317
1931	51,347
1946	59,220
1960	90,505
1970	119,934
1980	145,353

Source: Belize censuses, 1946, 1960, 1970, 1980.

1945 to 1985, an accelerated growth rate has caused the population to more than double (see Table 3.1).

Since a net emigration has taken place from Belize in this century, the high growth rate has resulted chiefly from a natural increase. The birth rate has remained high, around forty per thousand, whereas the death rate has declined, from about nineteen per thousand in the 1930s to less than five per thousand today. In particular, the dramatic decline in the infant mortality rate—from 190 per thousand in the 1930s to 93 per thousand in the 1950s, to less than 30 per thousand in the 1980s—has resulted in the high rate of natural increase and a population of which about 46 percent are aged fourteen years or less. Though the population grew by over 50 percent between 1946 and 1960, the average annual rate of increase has declined, from just over 3 percent between 1946 and 1960 to just under 2 percent since 1970. At this rate, the population of Belize would be well over 200,000 by the year 2000, but the large-scale migration of Belizeans to the United

States, and of people from neighboring countries into Belize in recent years, makes predictions very difficult.

Immigration, which provided the origins of the Belize population in the eighteenth and nineteenth centuries (see Chapter 2), has increased again in recent years. The proportion of foreign-born Belizeans declined steadily from 57 percent in 1861 to 7.8 percent in 1960. Then, as thousands of Mennonites, Mexicans, and Central Americans came to Belize in the 1960s and 1970s, the foreign-born proportion increased to about 11 percent in 1980. Most recently, an influx of several thousand refugees has occurred as a result of the wars in Central America: Between 1980 and 1983 about 5,000 refugees from Guatemala and El Salvador settled in Belize. According to the most recent estimates (August 1985) there are between 15,000 and 20,000 refugees in Belize. Overall, however, there has probably been a net emigration in the past two or three decades, as at least 20,000 Belizeans have settled in North America, chiefly for economic reasons.

Although the overall population density is about seventeen per square mile, some districts are much more densely populated than others, and a high degree of urban concentration is present. Belize District, which contains over one-third of the total population, has about thirty-two persons per square mile, but Toledo District is more scarcely populated with seven persons per square mile.

Since about 1930, over half the population of Belize has been living in the seven largest towns, which, in order of decreasing size, are Belize City, Orange Walk Town, Corozal Town, Dangriga, San Ignacio, Benque Viejo, and Punta Gorda. Since 1970, the new capital, Belmopan, has grown into a town of over 3,000 people, but Belize City, with about 40,000 people, remains the chief urban center. Belize City is very congested, noisy, dirty, and often oppressively humid; yet, with its sea breezes and lively bustle, it is not unattractive. Because of its unusual location, bounded by the sea and swampy ground, the city cannot easily expand, and its growth rate has slowed in recent years in relation to other urban areas. Orange Walk Town is growing especially rapidly, from 1,099 people in 1931 to 2,157 in 1960 and 8,439 in 1980.

Children of Belize

What is surprising, especially in comparison with the experience of increasing urbanization in other countries, is that the proportion of the total population that lives in the towns has declined recently and is scarcely more now (51.7 percent) than it was in 1931 (51.4 percent).

Almost half of the population of Belize still inhabits rural areas, living in small villages and hamlets around Corozal and Orange Walk Towns in the north, along the Belize River and Western Highway, on the coast south of Belize City, and in southern Toledo District. Much of the rest of the country—the northwest region, the coast north of Belize City, and much of southern Cayo and northern Toledo Districts—is very thinly populated. From the air or driving through the country at night, it is striking how much of Belize remains a forested wilderness, crossed by an occasional unpaved road or inhabited by scattered farms and logging camps. Unlike many Caribbean countries, then, Belize is not densely populated, does not suffer from uncontrolled urban growth, and retains considerable underdeveloped rural resources. Since during the late classic period the area that is now Belize supported more than twice the present population, with suitable development the country clearly can continue to grow for a long time without becoming overpopulated.

CULTURAL DIVERSITY

Because the majority of Belizeans are descendants of immigrants from various homelands, the small nation has an astonishingly diverse culture. We can begin to examine this phenomenon by studying census data on race, language, and religion. As these categories overlap in some important ways, it becomes clear that, although some quite distinct ethnic communities exist in Belize and the members of these communities are unevenly distributed through the country, a summary of such a complex society runs the grave risk of oversimplification.

The earliest enumerations in the late eighteenth and early nineteenth centuries failed to count the Maya and Garifuna people and classified the population as slave or free, the latter being subdivided into "black," "coloured," and "white." Whites never made up more than 10 percent of the population after 1790, but the free colored population increased from 15 percent in 1816 to 26 percent in 1832 and the free blacks from 10 percent in 1816 to 22 percent in 1832. According to the slave register of 1834, 91 percent of the slaves were blacks, the rest being of various mixed categories. The population at the time of emancipation, therefore, not counting the Maya and Garifuna, consisted of approximately 61 percent blacks, 30 percent colored or mixed, and 9 percent white.

The first modern census, in 1861, classified the elements of the population in a way that is hard to decifer, but its results suggest that perhaps 18 percent were Maya, 38 percent Mestizo, 10 percent African or black, 21 percent colored, 4.5 percent white or Spanish, and 7 percent Garifuna, the remainder being East Indian, Chinese, or not stated. The 1946 census enumerated the "races," using a jumble of biological, cultural, and national categories: American Indian, 17 percent; white, 4 percent; black, 38 percent; East Indian, 2 percent; Carib, 7 percent; mixed, 31 percent; Syrian, Chinese, and not stated, 1 percent. The 1980 census is somewhat more precise in its classification by race. Of the two chief groups, Creoles now constitute 40 percent of the population and Mestizos, 33 percent. Next come the Garifuna with 8 percent, the Maya with 7 percent, white with 4 percent, Kekchi with 3 percent, and East Indian with 2 percent. These ethnic groups are unevenly distributed throughout the country, and some groups are concentrated in certain locales. Several larger towns have a particular ethnic character; for example, Belize City is 76 percent Creole, Dangriga is 70 percent Garifuna, and Orange Walk Town is 69 percent Mestizo. But some smaller villages have the strongest ethnic identity, such as the Kekchi and Garifuna communities in the south and the Mennonite settlements in the north and west.

In general, the present geographical distribution of ethnic groups reflects their history and their settlement when they entered the country. Thus, the Creole community is still concentrated in Belize City and the surrounding region, the Mestizos are largely in the north, the Garifuna in coastal communities in the south, the East Indians in rural Corozal and Toledo, the Kekchi in rural Toledo, and the Mennonites in the villages in Cayo and Orange Walk Districts where they settled soon after arriving in 1958. In some cases a virtual segregation of an ethnic group occurs; for instance, almost all the Kekchi are in a few small, self-contained villages in rural Toledo. However, considerable interaction and interpenetration also take place between these groups; for example, the Garifuna, though only 8 percent of the population, are present in every part of Belize, rural and urban.

The very fact that Belize is unusually racially and culturally heterogeneous even for a Caribbean or Central American country tempts the observer into oversimplified characterizations. For example, the distinguished anthropologist M. G. Smith has described Belize as divided between the worlds of the "Negro-white Creole" and the "Spanish-Indian mestizo," in what he calls a "cleavage . . . culturally, linguistically, and by race."[1] However, an examination of particular cultural characteristics, such as language and religion, shows that these attributes overlap and cut across ethnic and racial distinctions, thus uniting as well as distinguishing people in different ethnic groups throughout the country.

English is the first language of a little over one-half the people of Belize, and Spanish is the first language of just under one-third. The remainder grow up speaking a variety of languages, including Garifuna, Maya (Yucateco, Mopanero, and Kekchi), and low German. English is the first language for nine out of ten people in Belize District but for less than one in five people in Corozal and Orange Walk Districts, where Spanish is the primary language of about 70 percent of the people. Belize appears to have a kind of mosaic of languages, but perhaps as many as one-third of the Belizeans are bilingual and even trilingual. English is the official language and the language of instruction in the schools, so many Spanish, Maya, and Garifuna speakers can also speak English. Perhaps about 80 percent of the population can speak English. Most Maya are hispanicized through long contact with the Spanish culture of Mexico or Guatemala, and many Garifuna speak English and Spanish as well as their own language.

St. John's Cathedral, Belize City; consecrated in 1826

In the first half of the twentieth century the proportion of Belizeans for whom English was the primary language increased from about 53 to 60 percent while the Maya and Kekchi speakers declined from 15 to 10 percent. The latter decline has continued, but the proportion of people whose first language is Spanish has increased from 22 percent in 1946 to 32 percent in 1980, chiefly because of recent migration patterns. On one hand, about one in five of the foreign-born population in 1980 came from Mexico, Guatemala, Honduras, and El Salvador, and the number of refugees from Guatemala and El Salvador has increased dramatically since then. On the other hand, most of the thousands of Belizeans who have settled in North America are English speakers. Even though English and Spanish will remain the most widespread languages, it is to be hoped that, as more Belizeans become bilingual and even trilingual, the use of minority languages will not decline further.

The pattern of religion in Belize is less of a mosaic than that for language because three of every five people are Roman Catholic and they make up a majority in every district except Belize. A large number of different Protestant sects are represented: The Anglicans and Methodists are currently the most numerous, but their numbers are declining as the Pentacostal and Adventist churches gain adherents. The Anglican was the first established church and was incorporated into the Jamaican diocese in 1824. It was disestablished along with the Presbyterian church in 1872, and the number of Anglicans has recently declined from 21 percent of the population in 1946 to less than 12 percent in 1980. The first Baptist missionary arrived in 1822, followed by Wesleyan Methodists in 1825. These missionaries competed to baptize, bury, and sometimes even marry the slaves, but, with the exception of the Methodists who worked among the Garifuna (they are still strong in Dangriga), most missionary activities and congregations were limited to Belize Town. Today, only 6 percent of the population is Methodist, and the Baptists claim less than 1 percent, most in Belize District. Pentacostal evangelicals have had some success, particularly in Toledo and Cayo Districts, and the Mennonites, who mostly keep their congregationalist Protestantism to themselves, are now the fourth largest religious community in Belize.

The influx of refugees from Yucatán gave rise to the first Catholic church in 1851 (if we discount the Spanish missionary efforts in the seventeenth century), and in 1956 Belize became a Catholic bishopric. The Catholic Church has grown in part because it has gained many adherents among the Creole people, as well as among the Garifuna, Maya, and Kekchi. The Catholic religion is not limited to a particular ethnic community in Belize but is a national institution that overlaps and cuts across ethnic groups, uniting 61.7 percent of the population in one denomination. The visit of Pope John Paul II to Belize on 9 March 1983 was a truly national event, though he never left the international airport. He was greeted by 15,000 people, including the heads of the Anglican and Methodist Churches as well as the Roman Catholic Bishops, and, symbolically, received gifts from members of eight Belizean ethnic groups.

Although it is possible to identify the two large communities in Belize as the Creole and Mestizo complexes—the former combining whites, Creoles, and Garifuna, and the latter consisting of Spanish, Mestizo, and Maya—this analysis is too static and simple by far.[2] When so many Creoles and Garifuna share Catholicism with Mestizo and Maya and when English-speaking people belong to many different religious denominations, the definition of these so-called complexes becomes elusive and a hindrance to understanding Belizean culture. Although language and religion are two of the chief ways in which people relate to each other and identify themselves, and hence are important aspects of ethnicity, they are themselves parts of a very complex process that contributes to the cultural history and future of Belize. Knowing how many people speak which languages and participate in which churches aids the understanding of Belizean culture only if culture is viewed as a dynamic process, sustained and transformed by the daily activities of individuals in multifarious relations with other individuals.

NATIONAL UNITY

Belizeans interact in many ways, within a wide range of activities and institutions that promote national unity. This is not to say that Belize will soon, or ever, become culturally homogeneous; nor is that a goal that any Belizean seeks. Rather, the emergence of Belize as a nation from the colonial crucible has both reflected and promoted important activities and institutions in which Belizeans share and take pride, and that, in a common cultural process, promote their identity as Belizeans. When a British historian published a study of British Honduras in 1961 before self-government had been achieved, he doubted the potential for national unity. The "Spanish," he argued, "present the real difficulty in the way of British Honduran unity. It is possible that, if British Honduras were to become independent, a national feeling and a loyalty wider than the present communal ones might develop. It is not altogether inconceivable that at some time in the future an integration of 'creole' and 'Spaniard' could take place."[3] Now that independence has been achieved, national unity is closer, but the integration that is developing is not conceived under the umbrella of a British Honduras. Such a conception assumes that the British heritage is somehow paramount, leaving minorities to make the adjustments to achieve national integration, and resulting perhaps in the kind of persistent unease that exists in Canada (or in Britain itself). The model of Belizean nationalism appears, rather, to be one of cultural pluralism, a model that acknowledges the value of the diverse cultural heritages that constitute Belize and provide its unique national identity.

Among those important activities and institutions that unite Belizeans of different cultures is education, which plays a key role in the decolonization process. The history of education in Belize shows that it is capable of promoting either unity or diversity, conformity or conflict, and its role in the near future is by no means certain. On one hand, most schools, particularly primary level ones, are still denominational and hence are in danger of being more concerned with teaching the particular beliefs and values of a church and with recruiting and maintaining its congregation than with furthering the more universal ideas and values associated with national unity. On the other hand, since the classes are still officially conducted in English, the danger exists that that language will be used to promote the dominance of one cultural heritage over the minorities, thus advancing national unity at the expense of cultural diversity. The general thrust of the Belizean education system in this regard is unclear, but the government is apparently giving greater emphasis and assistance to education in the 1980s than in the past, when government aid was provided but education was left in the hands of the various churches.

According to the 1980 census, 92 percent of the adult population is literate and 85 percent of school-age children attend primary school. The number of government and government-aided primary schools has increased from 139 in 1965, with 25,268 pupils enrolled, to 196 in 1982, with 35,081 enrolled. Of these 196 primary schools, 113 are managed by Catholics (22,242 pupils), 23 by Anglicans (4,125 pupils), and 22 by Methodists (3,263 pupils). Enrollment in secondary education, which remains a privilege for a minority, increased from 3,647 students in 1970 to 5,522 in 1982, with another 567 enrolled at the Belize Technical College.[4] In 1982, there were twenty-two secondary schools and five other, more specialized colleges, including the teacher's college, agricultural school, and nurse's school.

As the newly independent country adapts its colonial education system to its own needs, technical, vocational, and agricultural training are increasingly emphasized. One already quite successful program, Relevant Education for Agriculture and Production (REAP), is directed toward providing a favorable orientation toward agriculture and associated practical subjects in the primary schools. Until recently, secondary educational institutions were mostly located in Belize City, but new secondary schools have been established in the districts. The government has also been actively promoting preschool education and has established the Belize College of Arts, Science and Technology (BELCAST) to focus on higher education in Belize. For many years a contributor to the University of the West Indies, which has a university center in Belize City, Belize has sent students to Jamaica, Trinidad, and Barbados to obtain degrees, as well as to Britain, the United States, Canada, and, recently, Cuba.

The result of these efforts is almost universal primary education (85 to 90 percent of all children complete eight years of primary schooling) and an expanding and more egalitarian secondary-school system, but higher education remains the privilege of a tiny handful. Census figures of educational attainment show that few differences exist between men and women, except that slightly more men complete university education.

The fact that education is increasingly linked to occupations means that the paucity of opportunity for training in professional and technical skills bodes ill for Belize's economic development. A mere 3.5 percent of adults (fifteen years and over) have professional and technical training, and 9 percent of the labor force works in that occupational sector, mostly in Belmopan and Belize City. Agriculture, forestry, and fishing continue to be the most important sectors, employing a third of the labor force, much of it in seasonal wage labor, subsistence farming, or a combination of the two, that can support only a poor standard of living. Industry is still poorly developed, but, along with transportation, it accounts for about 24 percent of the labor force. Although occupations in industry and agriculture employ mostly males, the service, sales, and clerical sectors employ more women; as a result female participation in the labor force has increased from 20 percent in 1960 to 30 percent in 1980. As the participation rate of males has remained at about 98 percent, the percentage of the working-age population in the labor force has increased from 58 percent in 1960 to 65 percent in 1980. If the labor force continues to grow at this rate, the economy will have to grow more than 6 percent a year simply to absorb the new workers entering the labor market. As will be seen in Chapter 4, many obstacles stand in the way of such growth, so it is likely that unemployment, which has risen from about 9 percent in 1960 to about 14 percent in 1980, will continue to grow. Part of the unemployment problem, however, results from the fact that many people, particularly those living in Belize City, have neither the appropriate attitude nor the training to work in agriculture, where employment opportunities still exist. The seasonal demand for labor in the sugar and citrus industries is generally met by about 1,500 guest workers from Mexico and Guatemala, whereas Belizeans migrate to the United States. So long as most agricultural work remains unattractive because it has low status, is merely temporary and insecure, and is poorly paid, this situation is likely to persist. The number of people employed full time for wages outside Belize City continues to be small, and the number of unemployed people in the city, now over 3,000, continues to rise.

Although the various ethnic groups in Belize continue to be associated with certain economic activities and some economic sectors are socially quite segregated, the economic system as a whole interrelates people of different cultural background and ethnic identity. Few economic issues in Belize are as racially or ethnically divisive as they are, say, in Guyana. This fact does not contradict the idea that the colonial elite kept the various ethnic groups separated in economic organization as in other spheres, and it certainly promoted, among other racial and ethnic stereotypes, prejudicial ideas about the kinds of work for which people were believed suited. Each group was thus encouraged to fear and envy the other groups, to feel they were better or worse than others, and all were taught to look up to the white or light brown elite of landowners and merchants who controlled the economy. But in this social pyramid there were few occasions for actual confrontation, so, although prejudices still persist, there is no tradition of interracial violence in Belize. Cultural and racial differences constitute obstacles to the development of working-class unity in Belize as elsewhere, but the economic organization and work environment of Belize are also parts of the *culture*, in the broadest sense, of all these ethnic groups. The obstacles and opportunities Belizeans face in the course of trying to develop their economy and improve their standard of living are parts of an experience that can promote either unity or division, depending on the nature of the responses they make to these problems.

The use of official sanctions and practices that favored racial prejudice and discrimination during the colonial era has now ended, but the consequences of these patterns persist in the social structure, as class distinctions are still correlated with race and ethnicity. Because of limited economic and educational opportunities little chance exists for social mobility, and the social pyramid remains very broadly based. Those who already have educational and economic advantages are generally able to ensure that their children will, at the very least, maintain their social position, whereas the number of people who have risen from the working class into the middle or elite ranks is still very small. Without major economic developments, it is unlikely that any really significant shifts will take place in the relations of class, race, and ethnicity in the social structure. The observation, made in 1960, that "the potential ability of the population was scarcely tapped, as there was no real outlet for it"[5] remains essentially true, despite the new secondary schools and expanding employment opportunities for women.

Only in the past fifty years have roads and other modern means of communication linked people from different parts of the country, and only in the past thirty years have the

expanding educational system and growing political participation enabled Belizeans from all social and cultural backgrounds to join in common national activities and institutions.
In many social activities, such as sporting events, holidays,
and funerals, as well as educational and economic activities,
people mix across class and ethnic lines. Party politics in
Belize, a phenomenon that dates from 1950, has not developed
along ethnic lines. Class factors as well as cultural differences
have been important in political behavior, as will be seen in
Chapter 5, and socioeconomic issues are coming increasingly
to the forefront of Belizean politics. Unless the recent influx
of Central American refugees is exploited to exacerbate ethnic
conflicts, the competition for power and resources involved
in opposing strategies of development will probably increasingly unite Belizeans of different cultural backgrounds in a
pattern more resembling class politics. But the processes of
political and cultural decolonization and of economic development are fraught with pitfalls that can provoke cultural
dissension as well as with opportunities to promote national
unity. Much will depend on the impact of external influences
and on the leadership of Belizean politicians and educators
in the 1980s.

CREOLIZATION

The Creoles of Belize are chiefly the descendants of the
slaves brought there in the eighteenth and early nineteenth
centuries, of subsequent immigrations of Africans or people
of African origin, and of the British settlers. Belize City is
largely a Creole community and over half of the Creoles in
the country live there; three-fourths of Belize District is Creole
and two-thirds of the country's Creoles live there. This
residential pattern reflects the historical situation and experience of this section of the population: urban-focused people
who worked seasonally in the forests. With the decline of
forestry, most Creoles sought urban occupations on the water-
front, in service industries, and in government jobs, and others
established small farms and villages along the roads and

rivers that provided transport into the Belize City market. In this context the Creole culture of Belize has emerged.

Creolization is a complex process of cultural synthesis in which the relations of Africans and Europeans, slaves, free people of color, and masters are the key determinants of the resultant culture. Because of this definition, any class- or status-segregated analysis of creolization must be inadequate: We should no more refer to the culture of the slaves than to the culture of the slaveowners as if these were autonomous cultures. The creolization process essentially refers to the interaction and interrelationship between these different kinds of people, out of which emerged a new culture, the origins of which lay in the heritages of Africa and Europe, but which is neither African nor European. As a general process, of course, creolization is common in the Americas, but the specifics vary from case to case and depend upon such factors as the longevity of the process and the ratio of the different groups in the population. In Belize, creolization began in about the 1720s when the first black slaves were imported, and within a few decades the slaves were the majority of the population.

Though people of African origin were the overwhelming majority of the population, their cultural heritage was suppressed by the dominant minority whose own culture made a disproportionate contribution. The British settlers' control over the economic and political administrative system of the incipient colony ensured the paramount influence of British culture in these domains, as in the areas of law, language, and religion. The Africans managed to resist the suppression of their heritage, however, and they were frequently successful at adapting to their new and adverse social conditions. The British settlers were also changed by this process, as they found it impossible or simply inconvenient to maintain many of their treasured British ways and manner of dress, speech, cuisine, and social relations.

The British masters commonly had slave mistresses and from these relationships sprang the colored population, some of whom were freed by their fathers. The growing free colored population was generally poor and depended upon the prin-

cipal inhabitants, but some became educated and wealthy—
some, indeed, became slaveowners themselves. Those whose
opinions and aspirations have survived in the archives were,
not surprisingly, more oriented toward their British heritage
and sought to emphasize their "whiteness" and their distance
from their African ancestry. Their social position was inferior
to that of the whites (for example, they could not become
magistrates or jurors, and, though after 1808 they could vote
in Public Meetings, their property and residence qualifications
were twice those of whites), and they petitioned for fuller
rights and privileges. The fact that some of the free colored
appealed to the people in power and sought to raise their
own status within the existing social hierarchy does not mean,
however, that all the free people of color joined the settler
elite in exploiting and despising the black majority. They
were, in any case, something of a bridge between the two
social and cultural poles of the society—the British masters
and the African slaves. The free colored were neither slaves
nor wholly free people, neither African nor British, black nor
white. They, perhaps more than any others, were Belizean
Creoles, and they were members of families and social net-
works that linked British with Africans in relationships that
helped create a Belizean Creole culture.

Though the slaves came from many different African
peoples, most of their cultures placed a great emphasis on
the importance of religion, and their religious leaders, who
were often also healers, judges, and teachers, were influential
people. The practice of obeah—a means for manipulating
and controlling the world, both natural and supernatural—
bridged the areas of religion and magic. Obeahmen claimed
exceptional knowledge of medicines, charms, and fetishes and
were frequently associated with rebellions. Consequently a
law was passed in Belize in 1791 making the practice of
obeah, by men or women, punishable by death. Obeah has
continued in Belize, however, and, as in other parts of the
Americas, it is sometimes resorted to by people who belong
to Christian churches, without apparent contradiction. Nevertheless, the influence of British missionaries and churches has
been profound, especially through the schools. Anglicans,

Baptists, Wesleyan Methodists, and Presbyterians were all busy baptizing and burying slaves in the 1820s (only Anglican marriages were legal in the settlement and they married few slaves and not many free blacks and colored). Though it is hard to estimate the extent to which African elements were synthesized with European beliefs and practices in these Christian churches, such creolization certainly occurred.

Music and dance were frequently intrinsic parts of religious ritual and magical practices in Belize as in Africa. Knowledge of how to make and play musical instruments survived the middle passage, and, despite efforts by the masters to suppress music that they considered a nuisance or an incitement to revolt, the slaves maintained much of their musical heritage by adapting to the new conditions and creating within their traditions. In Belize the gombay was referred to as a recreational event as well as the goat's skin drum that is played with the hand. The influence of these early gombays is still felt today in the music of "boom-and-shine" bands. Music and dance have long been means of defining a community's identity as well as personal expressions. Since men were separated from their relatives and friends for long periods in the forest, Christmas provided an opportunity for intense communal recreation. Early nineteenth century accounts refer to the vigorous dancing, the "bursts of loud chorus," boat races, flag dancing, and rivalry between "sets" or groups that identified themselves by tribal origins. Christmas is still a time of reunions, of coming together in Belize City, and of the loud, vigorous drumming and dancing known as the "bram."

Perhaps the clearest example of creolization is in the language itself. The masters gave slaves new names, often their masters', and they were taught the masters' language, along with work routines and authoritarian relationships. Masters tried to keep slaves of the same culture apart so that they could only communicate with each other in their masters' language and had few opportunities to use their own. Nevertheless, the masters were not wholly successful in deracinating their slaves. As in other creole languages of the Americas, Belizean Creole is a version of English in which some constructions and words are African. This creole language, the phonology, vocabulary, and syntax of which differs significantly from standard English, was the means of expression through which proverbs, sayings, and folktales conveyed African values and wisdom and often satirized the British elite. In "bruckdowns," a calypso-like composition, words are joined with music to tell a story, relate a local incident, or mock a prominent personality, and the singer-poets are praised for their wit and daring. Recently, some volumes of poetry and a novel, Zee Edgell's *Beka Lamb*,[6] suggest a ripening of Belizean literature. Few of the poems are in Creole, but the subject matter is generally local and frequently patriotic in tone. The novel portrays a young Creole girl in Belize City in the 1950s, and the fact that it focuses on everyday aspects of family life, education, and the politics of the early independence movement asserts the importance of that subject matter in a newly confident manner. These are signs that the feelings of cultural inferiority the British instilled in the Creole elite are waning. Nationalism is prompting artists and educators to revalue their own folk arts, wherein the creative and resistant strains have long survived. A new pride in their creole culture, an eagerness to draw on African as well as European elements of their heritage, will encourage the development of increasingly distinctive Belizean arts. This is true of other cultures in Belize, also.

The cultures of the Maya, the Mestizos, and the Garifuna are all products of the synthesis of Old and New World cultures. Few of the Yucatec Maya now speak a Maya language; having been hispanicized rather than anglicized, they are mostly Spanish speaking and Catholic. Even the Kekchi, who maintain their own language, are influenced by Catholic missions and schools. The diet of all these Maya still follows the traditional emphasis on corn, beans, and chiles, however, and some ancient religious beliefs and practices persist. The Mestizos are generally more hispanic in their customs than the Maya, and their language and religion have distinguished them sharply from the Belizean Creoles. Nevertheless, in the twentieth century especially, these two cultural communities, the Mestizo and the Creole—themselves the outcome of

Garifuna celebrations in Dangriga

previous processes of cultural synthesis—have been mixing
and borrowing from each other. Tortillas and rice and beans
are both perceived as typically Belizean, and family, community, and seasonal festivities, along with schools and work
places, generally integrate these ethnic elements all over Belize.
It is now quite striking how culturally different the recent
Central American immigrants are from the Belizean descendants of the Yucatán refugees who arrived a century and
more ago.

    A quintessential case of cultural synthesis is surely the
Garifuna, whose culture is a product of Caribbean cross-
fertilization over centuries, a culture that is neither Carib nor
African, yet is derived from both, with European additions.
Their language is basically Carib, and their music and dance
are chiefly African in origin. The Garifuna in Belize have
retained the tradition of John Canoe, called by them *vanaraqua*,
which is known elsewhere in the Afro-Caribbean. At Christmas dancers, dressed in elaborate costumes with masks and
decorative headdresses, perform with drummers in the streets
of Punta Gorda, Dangriga, and Belize City. They include a
king, a clown, and several boys and men dressed as pregnant
women. The dancers, stepping quickly to the drums' poly-

rhythms, with arms outstretched, mock the white-faced, mustachioed European colonizers. In religion, too, even though most Garifuna attend Catholic or Methodist churches, they also maintain ancient beliefs and rituals, especially the ancestral rite, *dugu*, which is both the occasion and expression of their cultural identity. Traditionally, Garifuna make their living from fishing and most still live in the coastal communities of Dangriga, Punta Gorda, Hopkins, Seine Bight, and Barranco. Recently, farming has become more important among them, and many seek work outside their communities in Belize and the United States. Some of these—successful professionals who speak three languages—feel that their old ways are now threatened and are anxious that their children know what it means to be Garifuna. Like other Belizeans, such people are trying to be mobile and modern without being rootless and losing their valued heritage.

Finally, a contrast of the East Indians and the Mennonites shows how differently two small groups may be integrated into Belize. The few hundred Indians who were brought to Belize to work on sugar estates in the late nineteenth century lived in rural Corozal and Toledo Districts. Their descendants may still be found in communities like Calcutta near Corozal, but the Indians were so few, so poor, and so isolated from their cultural heritage that most of their original culture has been lost. Apart from a few traditional foods, these people have become so integrated that they can scarcely be distinguished culturally from the Creoles. This type of integration is precisely what the Mennonites are intent on avoiding. The Mennonites began arriving in Belize in 1958 when they were granted exemption from military service and any compulsory insurance or welfare schemes. They refrain from voting in national affairs and do not accept public office, preferring to maintain their three communities—at Spanish Lookout in Cayo and at Shipyard and Blue Creek in Orange Walk District—in political and cultural isolation. In economic affairs, however, they are very active and successful, mostly in the production and sale of poultry and dairy products. They teach their children German and their own form of Protestantism and maintain their distinct congregationist form of self-government. The more "open" community at Spanish Lookout has more social interaction than the others with local Belizeans, but in general these Mennonite settlements are unlikely to have much effect upon, or to be affected by, Belizeans. Indeed, unlike all the other peoples discussed, of whatever backgrounds, the Mennonites do not consider themselves Belizean. For most other people living in Belize, the creolization process has gone so far that they now think of themselves, in part at least, as distinctly Belizean, and ethnic identity is largely a matter of what people think they are, either in relation to, or regardless of, their cultural origins.

NEW INFLUENCES

Most influences upon the development of Belizean culture in the past have been through the immigrants who formed the society. For many immigrants, whether African, Garifuna, or East Indian, their place of origin was remote and there was little or no possibility of maintaining or renewing cultural contacts with their old country. For the British and the Mestizos, however, such a possibility existed, explaining in part why these two sources of cultural influence have remained important in Belize. Local versions of British and Spanish language, customs, and institutions remain the most widespread and influential throughout Belize. While the Spanish influence is being reinforced now through the influx of Central American refugees and access to goods and telecommunications from neighboring countries, the British influence is certainly waning. The influence of the United States, though not new, is now growing in importance and is increasingly visible in Belize, particularly in religion, consumer goods, and media.

The United States has long considered the Caribbean and Central America as its backyard, and, whether to control access to the strategic Panama Canal or to protect its growing business interests, the U.S. government has increased its influence in the region during the past century. By the 1880s, after several decades of diplomatic dispute concerning British settlements in Central America, the United States accepted

British sovereignty over Belize, and this fact shielded Belize from the U.S. political and military interventions that subsequently characterized the region. However, the growing U.S. economic influence in Belize, inevitable as the United States became a larger and more convenient market and source of supply than Britain, was related to its increasing cultural influence. When the subsidized mail route was changed in 1879 from a monthly service with Jamaica to a fortnightly service with New Orleans, the orientation of Belize's economy began to change. The development of the chicle and banana industries expanded trade with the United States, and by 1920 70 percent of all trade was with the United States, compared to only 16 percent with the British Empire. When after the 1931 hurricane the British government loaned $200,000 to the Belize Estate and Produce Company to open a sawmill, this action was partly to reduce the dependence of the forestry industry on U.S. buyers and to maintain British economic interests in Belize. The tide of trade could not be turned, however, and the exports of sugar, citrus, and seafood to the United States and the imports of various consumer goods increased in the 1960s. In May 1976 the link of the Belize dollar with sterling was broken, and it has since been tied to the U.S. dollar, at the rate of two to one. Over half of Belize's exports of domestic goods is now to the United States, and over a third of Belize's imports comes from that country.

Other ties with the United States have been immigration and emigration. The British encouraged Confederate refugees from the U.S. Civil War to settle in Belize in the 1860s. Governor John Austin is even reported as having told the U.S. consular agent that the only hope for the future of the colony was with such immigration and that if enough Confederates came Britain would grant Belize independence. Many such refugees came in the period from 1864 to 1870, but most went on to Guatemala or Honduras or returned to the United States. Of the few who remained in Belize, the most significant were those who formed the Toledo Settlement in the south. Started by a group of Southern Methodists in 1867, this estate near Punta Gorda had some 600 acres under cultivation by 1890 and employed about 300 workers, mostly producing sugarcane. Their unwillingness to mix with the local population (children were sent to white schools in the United States to avoid the dangers of miscegenation), their refusal to produce rum, and the decline in the price of sugar undermined the settlement, and by 1910 most Americans had gone home. Today, less than 7 percent of the foreign-born population was born in the United States, and many of these people are probably transient expatriates rather than settlers. However, the number of U.S.-born people, now over 1,000, is greater than the number of those from Canada and Britain combined and is more than four times what it was only twenty years ago. The influence of this minority is disproportionate to its number, as it was for the Baymen of yesteryear, because its culture has considerable economic and political support and penetrates the media and educational institutions in ways that help form the attitudes, tastes, and values of Belizeans.

Probably more important than the number of Americans in Belize, however, is the number of Belizeans in the United States, now reckoned to be about 20,000. During World War II thousands of Belizeans migrated to the United States to work on farms. Since then, a steady flow of Belizeans has entered the United States, often illegally, in search of work, and their remittances to relatives at home are substantial. Through their communications and examples these people have fostered among Belizeans a taste for the U.S. lifestyle in such matters as sports, popular music, and consumer goods.

More influential than migrants, either from or to the United States, however, are the U.S. media and teachers in Belize. Fifty years ago, Governor Sir Alan Burns warned that the United States, through the cinema, trade, and education, was making Belizeans "more American than British in their outlook."[7] He recommended more scholarships to English schools and universities, prizes in Belizean schools in English language, literature, and history, and visits by Belizean Boy Scouts to Britain—in other words, a tightening of cultural colonialism in order to bind the local elite more firmly to Britain.

Contrary to the direction advocated by Governor Burns, the Belizean government has been working at cultural decolonization, especially through the education system, and is concerned about the danger of cultural recolonization, especially through the mass media. A program to develop relevant and appropriate school textbooks and other teaching aids, written and published in Belize, has been quite successful; previously, most texts were obtained from British publishers and were believed to promote a colonialist viewpoint of Belizean history, culture, and society. The government supports archaeological projects and is trying to establish a museum. Promotion of sports at the community and national level and the expansion of educational services from preschool to higher education are also seen as necessary ways to preserve and develop Belize's cultural heritage. At a recent United Nations Educational, Scientific, and Cultural Organization (UNESCO) conference, the Minister of Education, Sports and Culture, Said Musa, drew attention to the concern over U.S. domination of the media, especially television: "In Belize today we experience the phenomenon of having direct U.S. satellite T.V. broadcasts in our homes twenty-four hours a day. This explosion of television and its cultural implications is thrusting upon Belizeans an awareness of the opportunities presented while at the same time challenging us with an urgent responsibility to ensure the integrity of our culture."[8]

Although the U.S. media are not the sole foreign influences in Belize, the fact that Belize has no television station of its own, only one radio station, and few local magazines and newspapers makes it highly vulnerable to the glossy U.S. media. Mexican influence is felt in the north of Belize through trade, television, and visits, and similar influence is felt from Guatemala in the western and southern districts that share its borders. Influence from the English-speaking Caribbean is also felt through the calypso and reggae music from Trinidad and Jamaica and through the increasing numbers of students who have returned from the University of the West Indies. Despite the long historical relationship with Britain, then, the current outside cultural influences on Belize are more from the United States and countries in the Caribbean and Central America.

SOCIAL CHANGES

The most dramatic changes in Belize since the 1930s have been in the economy, in the political and educational systems, and in the growth and urbanization of the population. These major changes have produced other social changes that are transforming the nature of the society, as the majority of people improve their living standards and have a say in the political and economic life of their country.

The health of Belizeans has been improving, partly as a result of improvements in nutrition and housing and partly as a result of better and more widespread health services. The fall in the death rate from about 19 per thousand in the 1930s to 11.5 per thousand in the 1950s, 6.8 per thousand in 1970, and 4.9 per thousand in 1980 has resulted largely from the decline in the infant mortality rate—from an appalling 190 per thousand live births in the 1930s to 93 per thousand in the 1950s, 51 per thousand in 1970, and 30 per thousand in 1980. The Ministry of Health promotes the strategy of primary health care, which emphasizes social and preventive services connected with improvements in living standards and working conditions, particularly for those most in need, such as children, expectant women, and poor people. Despite this strategy, some 85 percent of actual expenditure still goes for staffing and operating the secondary and tertiary levels of health care, especially in Belize City and the district hospitals. Belize now has nine hospitals and twenty health centers with 578 hospital beds (1982), and the number of doctors has increased from fewer than 30 in the 1960s to 55 in 1980 and 75 in 1982. Since independence, the Ministry of Health has gained support and assistance from various international agencies, including the Pan American Health Organization and the United Nations International Children's Emergency Fund (UNICEF), and foreign governments, notably those of Britain, Canada, France, and West Germany, and cooperation with regional countries, such as Jamaica, Panama, Costa Rica, and Mexico, continues to grow.

A new social security system was started in June 1981, designed and implemented with help from the International Labor Organization, and the first recipient received a pension three years later. In addition to pensions, the scheme provides short-term benefits, such as those for sickness and maternity, and pensions for injured persons. This scheme is a major achievement that will help Belize's workers in the future. For many years, of course, the workers have been helping themselves, through the trade union movement, that has now been active for over forty years, and through various cooperatives and credit unions.

The credit union movement in Belize has about 30,000 members in twenty-three unions with a total savings of over $14 million. The credit union idea and organization have helped spawn a variety of cooperatives for producing and marketing in the fishing, agricultural, and apicultural industries. The Belize Fisherman Cooperative Association is an especially successful example of this form of social organization. The fishing cooperatives, started in 1960, produce lobster, conch, shrimp, and fish, and provide a good income and standard of living for their members and communities. These cooperatives are obliged to sell a proportion of their product at controlled prices on the local market, and their products account for 11 percent of the domestic exports of Belize. The whole philosophy of the cooperatives offers a way for Belize to develop socially as well as economically without excessive reliance upon outside capital and by using appropriate technology. It also allows Belizeans to develop their own knowledge and management skills in their own enterprises, without simply remaining dependent wage earners in a dependent economy.

The trade union movement has been a response to the latter phenomenon. The development of trade unions in Belize, forbidden by law until 1941, was also inhibited by several factors inherent in the general economic situation and labor conditions of the workers. Most labor is unskilled, seasonal, and insecure and dominated by a few companies that have been able to determine wage rates, benefits, and working conditions. In other words, the situation of most workers in Belize has been essentially dictated by the nature of the dependent economy, and their union movement has been a struggle to overcome these inherent disadvantages. When the economy was totally dominated by forestry and by the Belize Estate and Produce Company in particular, the laborers needed unity and courage to achieve the most minimal improvements. Labor conditions in the 1930s, described in Chapter 2, were in many ways comparable to those a century earlier just after emancipation: payment in rations and tickets, exploitation by company stores, terrible housing and health conditions, and no legal rights for workers. Until 1943, laborers who failed to fulfill their labor contract were tried for criminal offenses, which carried such penalties as imprisonment with hard labor.

The first mass-based trade union, the General Workers' Union (GWU), was formed in 1943, and it grew to over 5,000 members in 1951. In 1947, this union fought a bitter strike at the Belize Estate and Produce Company's sawmill in Belize City until wages were raised from $1.20 to $1.90 a day. GWU President Clifford E. Betson urged a united labor front and a socialist movement in his New Year's message in 1948,[9] but, when the GWU threw its support behind the new People's United party (PUP) in 1950, it lost its autonomy. The success of the PUP depended upon GWU support; Betson was one of the members of the initial People's Committee at its inception in January, and the two organizations held joint meetings. By April, however, the middle-class leaders of the People's Committee (Nicholas Pollard, John Smith, George Price, and Philip Goldson) had taken over the leadership of the GWU, thereby strengthening the base of the political movement but making the GWU more vulnerable.

In 1952, George Price was the president of the GWU and secretary of the PUP, Leigh Richardson was secretary of education for the GWU and leader of the PUP, and Philip Goldson was corresponding secretary for the GWU and assistant secretary of the PUP. A split in the union in 1956 was followed by a division in the PUP. Pollard, supported by Price, formed the Christian Democratic Union, which soon claimed twice as many members as the GWU.

The subordination of union to political interests led to a general decline in trade union activity and membership. In 1961 the PUP attempted to recreate a trade union base by fostering regional unions under the control of district representatives, but these local organizations were too weak and dependent to be effective or to promote working-class solidarity on a national basis. Attempts to produce a national federation were followed by further splits and new unions, which were more the object of support by political parties than autonomous organizations that could themselves provide support. Today, some eight trade unions are active in Belize with a combined membership of about 6,000. Given an increase in unemployment and the persistent seasonal nature of much work, most workers are still poor and insecure, and their unions are poor and unstable. Belizean unions are only likely to increase in membership and strength if the wage-earning population sees them as associated with a wider social movement—comparable to the political movement of the early 1950s—that provides mutual strength and commitment to common goals.

Considerable restlessness and frustration have been apparent, especially among the youth, since the late 1960s, but such discontent has not as yet been focused and organized, as it periodically was between 1934 and 1954. This dissatisfaction reflects the fact that, despite the beneficial social changes that have occurred since the 1950s, aspirations and expectations have developed more quickly. Because decolonization was delayed over thirty years from the formation of the PUP to independence, Belize's emergence as a sovereign state was postponed until a time when hopes of higher levels of consumption coincided cruelly with international recession. Even if the investment climate remains favorable (and it may deteriorate as a result of the regional situation, regardless of the Belize government's policy), Belize has been hurt by the fall in the price of sugar and the decline of reexport trade with Mexico caused by that country's financial crisis. The vulnerability of Belize's economy makes it a potential victim of International Monetary Fund (IMF) "assistance programs." If austerity measures are taken in the near future (as the higher taxes and rates included in an economic recovery plan announced in June 1984 indicate), then Belizeans will be deprived. Belize's open economy is evinced by its large balance-of-payments deficits, averaging $80 million per year between 1979 and 1982, but this problem also reflects a pattern of preferences for imported consumer goods that has historically been promoted by the merchant class and more recently by mass media advertising. Aspirations for better health, housing, and education and for wider participation in the country's political, economic, and cultural activities can be more easily met than the unrealistic desires for a consumer lifestyle modeled on that of the U.S. middle classes. That particular Golden Fleece is likely to remain elusive, and the search for it would be a bitter and frustrating experience for Belizeans.

NOTES

1. M. G. Smith, *The Plural Society in the British West Indies* (Berkeley, University of California Press, 1965), p. 310.

2. See C. H. Grant, *The Making of Modern Belize: Politics, Society and British Colonialism in Central America* (Cambridge, Cambridge University Press, 1976), Introduction.

3. D.A.G. Waddell, *British Honduras: A Historical and Contemporary Survey* (London, Oxford University Press, 1961), p. 75.

4. *Abstract of Statistics 1982* (Belmopan, Central Statistical Office, 1983).

5. Waddell, *British Honduras*, pp. 77–78.

6. Zee Edgell, *Beka Lamb* (London, Heinemann, 1982).

7. Gov. Sir Alan Burns to Secretary of State, 3 December 1935, BA, Despatches Out, #323.

8. Said W. Musa, *Statement at the 22nd Session of the U.N.E.S.C.O. General Conference*, 4 November 1983 (Belize Government Information Service).

9. *Belize Billboard*, 3 January 1948.

4

The Economy

The economic history of Belize has been aptly described as "a classic of colonial exploitation, of taking away and not giving back. . . . Of all the wealth taken from the country practically nothing was put back in the way of permanent improvements and capital development."[1] The centuries of economic exploitation and stagnation produced widespread poverty and very limited opportunities. In the two decades since Belize has had full internal self-government, a serious attempt has been made to begin to reverse this pattern of colonial exploitation and to eliminate its legacies of poverty and inequality.

COLONIAL TIES AND TRADE

Not surprisingly, for three centuries Belize was run "for what could be got out of it": Its chief raison d'etre for three centuries was to produce wealth for Britain, chiefly through the export of timber. The British settlement at Belize was just a small part of a worldwide process of colonization that involved a system of exploitation in which investment, trade, and labor drained the wealth of the colonies to the metropoles. Though this process was not so clearly articulated in the case of Belize, which was not formally declared a colony until after the mercantilist phase of colonial expansion was over and Britain had become more interested in its possessions in Africa and Asia, Belize was nevertheless systematically exploited. In the Belizean economy, production followed the dictates of trade, as the British markets, merchants, and investors determined what Belizeans would produce and how much they would get for it. From time to time, the state of Belize's economy, and especially of government's revenue, depended also on the entrepôt trade, both illegal and legal, between Britain and Central America and recently Mexico. Belize's economy has been so inherently weak, through excessive reliance on the export of one or two primary products and on the importation of goods for almost every consumer need including food, that it has been and still is extremely vulnerable to fluctuations in international trade.

In the eighteenth century, Belize depended almost entirely upon the export of logwood, and after the 1770s mahogany, to Britain. When the logwood trade was severely depressed in the 1760s and 1770s, the slaves rebelled at least three times. The indebted settlers struggled to survive the economic crisis by trying to increase the amount of logwood exported to compensate for its falling value. In this situation the slaves had to work harder while their rations deteriorated. A few years after the largest revolt in 1773, the settlement was saved by the increasing demand for mahogany, which had already been exported for several years before the Convention of London made it legal in 1786. From then until the 1950s, the export of mahogany was the mainstay of the economy, but, because of the long periods of depression in the mahogany trade, this economy was largely stagnant for over a century. Moreover, the dominance of the mahogany trade and the forestry industry in the ownership of land and in the colonial decision-making process retarded the development of agriculture and the diversification of the economy until very recently.

Belize's economy, though open, has been effectively limited to two traditional trading partners, first Britain and then, increasingly, the United States. The persistent ties to these industrial countries and the paucity of wider trading arrangements have reinforced the vulnerability of the economy. A shift in demand for a single product in one major market can have a shattering effect in Belize, and the tendency of manufactured and processed goods to rise in price relative to the goods that Belize exports has contributed to Belize's balance-of-payments problem. Current account balance-of-payments deficits have varied over the last few years, largely because of sharp fluctuations in sugar export earnings, from about 5 percent to about 20 percent of gross domestic product (GDP), averaging about 13 percent. These deficits are met mainly by official capital inflows in the form of grants and loans, and also private foreign investments and cash remittances from Belizeans abroad. If the prices of exports, especially sugar, citrus, and bananas, and the value of the reexport business continue to fall as they did in the early 1980s as a result of the international recession, Belize could be forced into obtaining loans from the IMF. (In June 1984, government officials presented their economic recovery plan, including major revenue measures, to the IMF and World Bank, in the expectation of receiving assistance.)

The range of commodities exported from Belize has become broader since World War II, as agriculture and fishing have largely replaced forestry. Around 1950, forest products, chiefly mahogany logs and lumber, chicle, and pine lumber, still accounted for about 85 percent of the total value of exports. Sugar production in the north and citrus production in the Stann Creek District quickly expanded in the 1950s, however, and since 1959 both sugar and citrus exports have exceeded that of forest products. In addition to sugar and molasses, citrus fruit, segments, juices, and concentrates, and mahogany and cedar, Belize now exports bananas and fish products, including lobsters, conch, and shrimp. Other exports include garments (though the local value added to that of imported materials is quite low), honey, and meat. While the value of sugar and molasses exported fell from 61 to 54 percent of total domestic exports between 1980 and 1983, the value of citrus and fish exports rose from 8 to 11 percent and 5 to 11 percent, respectively. After the 1980 boom the economy slumped until exports picked up again in 1983.

Although this shift from the traditional dependence upon the export of forest products to a range of agricultural and fishing products is an important diversification of the economy, Belize's balance-of-payments performance is still largely dependent on the prices and production of a very few products.

Between 1978 and 1983, the value of sugar and molasses, citrus, and fish ranged between about 70 and 79 percent of total export earnings. Since sugar prices are very unstable and banana prices are generally declining, Belize must look to expanding production of citrus, meat, honey, fish, and other products, such as rice, beans, and fruit, as well as export-oriented industries, in order to improve its trade situation.

Another way Belize can improve its balance-of-payments situation, of course, is by curbing imports, a difficult step, however, since many of these imports are essential for development and for consumption needs. Belize's heavy reliance upon imports, even imported foods that could be produced locally, is part of its colonial legacy. Belizeans have developed consumption patterns, encouraged by the merchant class and now by mass media advertising, that favor expensive imported to local goods, even when the latter are better quality. However, even if these consumption patterns change, two major problems would remain. First, Belize depends upon imported oil for its fuel supplies. Good prospects exist for finding oil and gas in Belize, but the search has so far been unsuccessful, and there is the possibility of developing solar, wind, and hydro power. The fuel bill has increased from about 5 percent of the total value of imports prior to the 1973 rise in prices to between 16 and 18 percent in the early 1980s. Second, many consumption goods cannot be profitably produced in Belize in competition with U.S. mass production, and the local market is so small. Only by increasing the size of the market (for example, through trade with Caribbean Economic Community, CARICOM, countries), employing appropriate technology (that does not itself require expensive imports of equipment and fuel), and changing consumer preferences can Belize successfully develop import-substitution industries. The clearest area in which to reduce imports remains food, which still constitutes about a quarter of the total value of imports.

Another way for Belize to improve its terms of trade is by seeking better deals with more diverse trading partners. Goods are chiefly imported from the United States and Britain, and although imports from other countries, such as Mexico,

Holland, and Japan, have been increasing, Belize is not always able to purchase consumer goods from the cheapest suppliers. The amount of imports from CARICOM countries is very small (about 2 percent of the total, chiefly from Jamaica), and for political reasons Belize is restrained from trading with countries like Cuba. The minister of economic development was reported as saying in 1984 that Cuba was "offering us refrigerators at half the price we were then paying for those we imported, but because of the whole paranoia about Cuba no businessman would touch them. The U.S. and Russia make deals about grain, but Belize cannot have any trade with Cuba."[2] So long as Belize exports most of its goods to the United States and Britain, those countries will probably retain considerable influence over where Belize purchases imports. The share of Belize's exports of domestic goods to these two countries has increased from about 69 percent in 1970 to about 81 percent in 1980. Currently, more than half of Belize's exports of domestic goods goes to the United States largely because of an increase in sugar exports, and Britain takes about 27 percent.

Belize continues to make money by reexporting goods, that is, by importing goods to Belize and then selling them in neighboring countries, as well as by transshipping goods and charging fees for port and road facilities. These operations were increasing rapidly until 1982 when the Mexican economic crisis sharply reduced such trade. Belize earns relatively little from tourism, which remains undeveloped by most Caribbean standards, but receives considerable transfers from the British Army stationed in Belize and remittances from Belizeans living abroad, both of which help fill the gap in the balance of payments. Such stopgap assistance cannot solve the problem, however, for it is inherent in the patterns of trade and the kinds of production and consumption that Belize has inherited from its colonial past. Such patterns will persist unless Belize can reduce the importation of nonessential items and produce substitutes for as many others as is practical, and expand and diversify its exports. In a situation of international recession and in particular of a crisis in the sugar market and of losses in the reexport trade with Mexico, it is

to Belize's credit that it survived its first years of independence
at all. To make progress in improving the living standards
of all Belizeans will now be a herculean task, one that requires
a long-term restructuring of the economy.

LAND, FORESTRY, AND AGRICULTURE

After emancipation, in many parts of the Caribbean
large numbers of former slaves, some of whom had engaged
in the cultivation and marketing of food crops, became a
real peasantry. The alternative was to remain dependent upon
their former masters, in a wage-earning, proletarian position.
Whether the former slaves became peasants or proletarians
depended upon several factors, including the accessibility of
markets for peasant produce. The chief factor was the avail-
ability of land, which was determined, not by simple population density but by the power structure. Belize, like Jamaica,
Trinidad, and Guyana, had a low population density in 1838;
yet a peasantry did not emerge in Belize as it did in the
other colonies in the middle of the nineteenth century. The
masters in Belize were more successful in controlling the labor
of their former slaves because they used a variety of measures
to make the wage earners indebted and keep them dependent,
including the monopoly of land ownership and the denial of
land to the former slaves. The land monopoly and the dominance of forestry inhibited the emergence of a peasantry
after emancipation and retarded the development of agriculture.[3]

Land ownership, already concentrated in the hands of
a few settlers by the end of the eighteenth century, became
consolidated still further in the depression in the mid-nineteenth century, as described in Chapter 2. The Laws in Force
Act and the Honduras Land Titles Acts, passed between 1855
and 1861, encouraged British investors and promoted the
growth of the British Honduras Company which, as the Belize
Estate and Produce Company since 1875, has been the chief
landowner and business enterprise in Belize for a century.
Until the 1960s, this company owned about 1 million acres
of the 2.3 million that were privately owned, and almost all

this gigantic estate was unused or exploited only for its natural forest resources. The Belize Estate and Produce Company never used proper forest management to conserve or replace trees, and, since mahogany is a slow and sparse growing tree, the reserves became seriously depleted, especially after new technology permitted extraction from more remote areas after the 1920s. The first Forest Department was established in 1922 after a report recommended intensive forest management to conserve and sustain yields, but legislation was not introduced until 1944. By that time, uncontrolled felling on private lands, aided by the revolution in transport and the roads built by the government in the 1930s, had made the creation of forest reserves more urgent.

The dominance of forestry interests was felt through the nineteenth century and the first half of the twentieth in the suppression of agriculture, the oppression of poor peasants and exploited forest workers, and the highest councils of the colony. Except for a brief period in the 1860s and 1870s when the British Honduras Company and some other large landowners invested in sugar cultivation, forestry remained the chief activity of the big landowning companies. The Belize Estate and Produce Company could not use all its million acres, of course, but it prevented others from using the land to keep the population dependent and so to ensure that it had a cheap labor force. Maya villages and *milpas* were destroyed on British Honduras Company lands in the Yalbac Hills in 1867 because the Maya were perceived as a nuisance to mahogany cutters and a potential labor force for agricultural plantations rather than as the pioneers in small farming that they in fact were. The governor issued a regulation in 1867: "No Indian will be at liberty to reside upon or occupy, or cultivate any land without previous payment or engagement to pay rent whether to the Crown or the owner of the land,"[4] and the following year Governor Longden agreed that the Maya should not be allowed to own land at all. In the 1930s, the Belize Estate and Produce Company drove the Maya from their villages of San Jose and Yalbac and treated its workers in the mahogany camps in ways reminiscent of slavery. The manager of the company was almost automatically a member of the Legislative Council and hence the company's influence on the colonial policy and administration was always strong. When the government increased the land tax to $.025 per acre in 1931, the large landowners refused to pay the tax. The government accepted some almost worthless land in lieu of taxes and in 1935 capitulated completely, reducing the tax to its former rate of $.015 per acre and annulling the large landowners' arrears by making the reduction retroactive to 1931. Since small landowners had meanwhile paid their taxes, often at $.30 an acre and more, this action by the government and the large landowners was clearly discriminating in favor of big forest interests against small farmers.

The Belize Estate and Produce Company survived the depression years because of its influence not only with the local colonial administration but also with the British government. Since 1875, various members of the Hoare family had been principal directors and maintained a controlling interest in the company.[5] Sir Samuel Hoare, a shareholder and former director, was secretary of state for air in 1928 and a friend of Leo Amery, the secretary of state for the colonies. In 1931, when the company was suffering from the aftereffects of the hurricane as well as the depression, another Hoare raised with the Colonial Office the specter of disposing of the company to U.S. buyers.[6] The British government rescued the company, which appeared synonymous with the economy at that time, by granting it a virgin area of mahogany forest and a loan of $200,000 to erect a sawmill in Belize City. When C. H. Brown, the expatriate manager of the company, was defeated by Robert Turton, the Creole chicle millionaire, in the first Legislative Council elections in 1936, he was promptly appointed to the council by the governor, presumably to maintain the influence of what had for so long been the colony's chief business.

Brown's defeat by Turton, one of the company's chief local business rivals, was a sign of changing times, the decline of the old British enterprises, and the rise of new Creole entrepreneurs linked with the more vigorous world of U.S. commerce. In 1947, the Belize Estate and Produce Company became a subsidiary of J. Glicksten Property and Investment

Trust Ltd., a giant transnational corporation that subsequently became part of the British-based conglomerate, International Timber Corporation,[7] whose 7,000 shareholders would have little interest in Belize or Belizeans. In the 1950s, forest products constituted about three-quarters of the value of all exports, and the industry employed some 3,000 workers in a total labor force of about 20,000. Today, it employs less than 1,000 workers in a labor force of over 46,000 people. Of the 10.6 million feet of lumber produced in 1983, 4.8 million were exported, earning $2.7 million, or only 2 percent of all exports. After three centuries of varied fortunes, the forest industry ceased to be the center of the economy and the Belize Estate and Produce Company, once the beneficiary and now the neglected subsidiary of international capitalism, began to relinquish some of its vast lands to the Belize government in lieu of taxes.

At the end of World War II the distribution of land was virtually the same as it had been in the late nineteenth century, and land taxes were the same as they had been in 1920. Some of the large estates changed hands, however, as U.S. landowners purchased them, often for speculative rather than productive purposes. In 1927, about 6 percent of the landowners, those with estates of 1,000 acres and more, held 97 percent of the freehold land, and in 1971 only 3 percent of the landowners held over 94 percent of the freehold land. At the other end of the scale, those farmers who owned 100 acres or less constituted, in 1927, 85 percent of the landowners with only 1 percent of the freehold land, and in 1971, 91 percent of the landowners with a mere 2 percent of the freehold land. These gross inequalities are sharpened by the fact that in 1971 all but one of the landowners with estates of 10,000 acres or more were foreigners. In fact, foreigners owned 93.4 percent of all estates of over 100 acres and over 90 percent of all the freehold land in Belize, with the Belize Estate and Produce Company alone in possession of about 42 percent.

Of approximately 5.6 million acres of land in Belize, some 2.2 million are considered suitable for agricultural development. A series of laws and incentives initiated by gov-

ernment in the past two decades is aimed at promoting
agricultural development. Although several attempts were
made earlier in this century, big landowners resisted taxation
increases and most agricultural development made use of the
plantation system, produced one or two crops for export to
fluctuating markets, and employed Belizeans as seasonal wage
workers. Only since the 1960s has the government more
systematically attempted land reform and agricultural diversification in an effort to make lands available to the farmers
prepared to use them. Through legislation and taxation the
government has sought to penalize the owners of large tracts
of undeveloped lands and to redistribute such land, when
possible, to progressive farmers. The attempts to tax undeveloped estates have not been very successful because large
landholders have the influence to obtain exemptions and find
loopholes.

A land acquisition ordinance, dating from 1947, gave the
government the authority to acquire land for public purposes
and to receive land from the large landowners in lieu of
taxes, but it was hard to find a means to push through the
necessary land reform while making all acquisitions seem
reasonable and giving equitable compensation. In 1962, a
security of tenure law was passed, but it only required the
landlord to give one year's notice before evicting a tenant
farmer and did nothing to provide the long-term protection
necessary to encourage agricultural development by small
farmers. The need to provide sound systems of tenure as
well as to transfer undeveloped private land to prospective
users was stressed in a UN report on the modernization of
agriculture in Belize written by René Dumont in 1963.[8] In
1966, the government passed the Land Tax (Rural Land
Utilization) Ordinance to levy tax on undeveloped rural lands
in parcels of over 100 acres, to encourage the owners either
to develop the land, or to dispose of it to those who would.
The minister introducing the bill, A. A. Hunter, saw it as a
progressive piece of legislation that could promote agricultural
development: "The Bill serves notice that from this day on,
breaking with the traditions of our past, we shall demand
from those in possession of our land a contribution to the

national welfare, commensurate with the privilege which they enjoy. It is an act of economic emancipation marking a watershed in our history."[9]

If the tax had been implemented, it would have discouraged the retention of land for speculative purposes by forcing the big landowners to develop their lands, pay large sums to the government, which could use them for development, or dispose of their land to the government in lieu of taxes. However, the Belize Estate and Produce Company acted in character by refusing to pay the new tax in 1967 and 1968 while lobbying for support in Belize and London. It achieved its objective in 1969, when it obtained exemptions from the tax for 967,754 acres, or about 95 percent of its rural lands. Another 262,060 acres, mostly owned by other absentee landlords, were also exempted. With 1.23 million acres exempted, the law was effectively subverted, and its intended effects were lost. Meanwhile, the relative contribution of the landowners to the national revenue declined. In 1868 the land tax collected as a temporary measure to help defray military expenses amounted to 8.3 percent of total current revenue, but in 1951 land taxes accounted for only 3.5 percent of current revenue, and in 1971 the combined land tax and rural land utilization tax produced a mere 2.4 percent of current revenue.[10] The aims of the Land Tax Act of 1982, which supersedes the previous taxes, are to raise revenue and to stimulate development by taxing the unimproved value of all lands without exemptions so as to discourage speculation and promote productive investments.

Another legislative step was taken in 1973 when the Alien Landholding Ordinance was passed regulating the right of foreigners to buy land and imposing conditions on their right to hold land. Foreigners must get a license from the Ministry of Natural Resources by showing how they will develop the land; the purpose of the law is to deter obvious speculation in favor of agricultural development. Within two years, over 100 licenses to nonnationals had been approved under this law, covering almost 200,000 acres, and defining certain conditions of development of the utilizable acreage within a ten-year period. In 1974, the law regulating the government's acquisition of land was revised to protect the public interest, for example, when the security of long-standing tenants was threatened. Despite such attempts to protect the interests of Belizeans and to promote agricultural development, however, most of the best arable land in Belize is still owned by foreigners and is still undeveloped. Between 1971 and 1975, the government distributed some 200,000 acres to Belizean farmers for development, and a further 325,000 acres were acquired for redistribution between 1975 and 1982.

The government now owns more than 1 million acres of land suitable for agriculture; much of it was received in lieu of taxes from large landowners, including the Belize Estate and Produce Company.[11] The government is currently implementing a rural development project on 15,000 acres in the Valley of Peace near Belmopan, for Belizean families and Salvadorean refugees. Each family receives fifty acres and pays no land tax for the first three years; any subsequent tax is set off against the purchase price. This project provides easy and cheap access to land for agricultural development. With projects such as these, Belize has begun the program of land reform and agricultural development necessary to escape the legacy of colonial dependency and land monopoly by creating a more self-sufficient and socially equitable economy.

As the pattern of land use began to change in the 1950s, the agricultural development that replaced forestry as the basis of the economy was dominated by foreign-owned plantations, especially in the production of sugar and citrus. Belize's modern sugar industry began in 1937 when a small factory was opened at Pembroke Hall, now Libertad, in Corozal District. Contractors, most of them foreign businesses with extensive estates, supplied the sugarcane. In 1964, the mill was bought and enlarged by the British corporation of Tate and Lyle, known in Belize as the Belize Sugar Industries Ltd. This company opened a large new factory at Tower Hill near Orange Walk Town in 1967, and thousands of acres in that district were planted in cane. By 1968, there were over 1,200 cane farmers in the northern districts, and nearly 67,000 tons

Tower Hill Sugar Factory, Orange Walk

of sugar were produced in 1970, most of it exported to Tate and Lyle's refinery in Liverpool.

In the 1960s, small farmers, who produced much of the cane sold to the factories, were threatened as the company began buying up private lands. Pressure from these farmers and the northern Cane Workers' Union, whose members' jobs were threatened by mechanized cane cutting, resulted in government action. As well as negotiating larger export quotas for sugar, the government guaranteed loans for small farmers to purchase their own land to create new cane fields. In 1972, because of the long conflict between Tate and Lyle and the farmers and workers, the company sold its plantations to independent Belizean farmers in a significant reversal of the usual process of plantation monopolization.

Most of the 4,000 farmers who now grow cane are small producers: Forty-five percent of them own less than six acres, their incomes are limited by their delivery licenses, and they often are indebted for their trucks and tractors. Many gave up all subsistence farming to expand cane production when sugar prices were high, and they are now dependent upon internationally determined prices and quotas that result in annually fluctuating incomes. Their standard of living has improved, but, as cars, trucks, and television sets change the character of the northern villages, much of the traditional culture is fading and, with the influx of migrant laborers and refugees from Mexico and Central America and an expanding drug trade, crime and violence are increasingly common.

Over 60,000 acres are now in cane cultivation, owned chiefly by the farmers. The region nevertheless is dependent upon international economic forces, and sugar production can be drastically affected by drought and disease. Only 62,000 tons were produced in 1975, when a severe drought hit the cane, but production reached a record 112,000 tons in 1978. Despite the International Sugar Agreement and the Lomé Agreement, Belize experiences sharp fluctuations in the average price it receives for sugar. In 1978, the average price was $592 per long ton, in 1980 it peaked at $982, and it has since dropped by about 35 percent. Tate and Lyle threatened to close the Libertad factory because it claimed to have been losing some $5 million a year since 1981. The government appointed a commission to study its proposals. Ironically, as soon as the once-thriving sugar industry faltered, the private transnational corporation invited nationalization.

The sugar industry has been the chief contributor to the Belizean economy since 1959, and the expansion of sugar production, from about 17,000 tons in 1959 to 114,000 tons worth $68.3 million in exports in 1983, has been a key element in the growth of the economy in the 1960s and 1970s. However, sugar, which accounts for between 20 and 25 percent of GDP, has suffered from drought, smut diseases, and frog-hopper infestation, as well as the fall in prices after 1980. Incomes of farmers and the Belize Sugar Industries (BSI) are tied directly to the price, the former receiving 65 percent and the latter 35 percent of the net value of the sugar sold. The fluctuating production and declining prices in recent years have certainly hurt the industry. The government agreed in 1984 to acquire 72 percent of the shares in BSI to add to the 3 percent it held previously through the Development Finance Corporation, leaving Tate and Lyle with 25 percent. This agreement was intended to save the Libertad factory, but in 1985 Tate and Lyle closed Libertad and laid off six hundred workers. It remains to be seen whether the sugar farmers themselves will purchase the shares in BSI and under what terms; if the company continues to lose $5 million a year they will not have gotten a bargain, but over 60,000 acres of the northern districts now seem to be committed to sugarcane.

At the moment Belize has a market for about 117,000 tons of sugar (9,000 tons locally; 41,000 tons to Britain; 30,000 tons to the United States; and 37,000 tons to the free market), which is more than it has been producing and slightly more than the current capacity of the two factories (115,000 tons). Since there is generally an overcapacity to produce sugar in the Caribbean, it would seem unwise for Belize to increase its capacity above 120,000 tons of sugar or to invest much more in a product subject to such sharp price fluctuations. The shareholders of Tate and Lyle, a multinational corporation with operations all over the world, could weather a crisis in the sugar economy in Belize, but 4,000 Belizean cane farmers and others whose livelihood depends upon them (over 1,000 people work in the factories, and about 5,000 extra workers are employed in crop season) could be ruined by a fall in sugar's fortunes. As the sugar crisis worsens it becomes increasingly clear that Belize must continue to diversify its agricultural base.

The citrus industry, based chiefly on the production of orange and grapefruit concentrates in Stann Creek District, is second to sugar as an agricultural export earner (and about equal now to fish products), responsible for 10.5 percent of the value of domestic exports in 1983 compared to sugar's 54 percent. A small citrus trade began in the 1920s, but the expansion of the industry, like that of sugar, occurred after World War II. Also like sugar, citrus has suffered from price fluctuations, and large increases in production have been required to offset a drop in prices of 30 percent since 1980. The Citrus Company of Belize, which has a little over 2,000 acres of orchards and an old factory at Pomona, was established by a Jamaican family that retains shares, but the major shareholder since 1984 has been the Cooperative Citrus Growers Association of Trinidad and Tobago. The 300 small farmers in the Belize Citrus Growers Association may buy shares in the company through the government's Development Finance Corporation. The other processor, Belize Foods Products, operates a plant built in 1963 and is a wholly owned subsidiary of Nestle's, the Swiss transnational company. Since 1979, the number of acres in citrus has expanded from 7,000 to 12,000, and production has increased from about 900,000 boxes in 1976–1977 to over 1.7 million boxes in 1981–1982, almost all of which is sold to Trinidad and Tobago. Though production slumped in 1983, exports of citrus products were worth $13.7 million, only slightly less than the value of the record crop in the previous year. The Commonwealth Development Corporation is pumping $6.4 million into the citrus industry through the Development Finance Corporation to help farmers expand and rehabilitate their orchards, and small farmers now produce about half of the total. So long as the citrus products enjoy the CARICOM and European Economic Community (EEC) markets, the prospects for the industry are good.

Banana production has a longer and less happy history in Belize. It started in the late nineteenth century but was ruined by the Panama disease. Rehabilitated with British aid in the early 1960s, it suffered from severe hurricane damage in 1975 and 1978, and production has declined in the last few years from 842,000 boxes in 1979 to 531,000 boxes in 1983. Exports to Britain, conducted by Fyffes, a subsidiary of United Fruit, have to go through Puerto Cortez, Honduras, in a costly arrangement. Improvement in port facilities could reduce transportation costs, and the industry could reasonably be expanded to about 4,000 acres, to supply 50,000 boxes per week, five times the present production level, in order to make it viable. An expansion of the banana industry is especially important as it would create much needed jobs in the south, which has a very high level of unemployment. The government is trying to support the industry and centralize the exports through a statutory body, the Banana Control Board.

Several other agricultural products have become well-established in recent years, notably, corn, rice, red kidney beans, beef, poultry, and honey, some of which are for domestic consumption and some for export. The honey industry, which is conducted on a small scale and organized cooperatively, earned $2.1 million in exports between 1979 and 1983; a record 543,000 pounds were produced in 1983. The production of beef, rice, and corn has fluctuated, but poultry and red kidney bean production has improved steadily since 1978. The shift in Belize's economy from the domination of forestry to a more diversified agricultural base has been quite dramatic in the last three decades. In 1950, forest products accounted for 85 percent of the value of total domestic exports and in 1981 for only 1.8 percent. In 1983, timber exports were valued at $2.7 million, compared with about $110 million worth of agricultural and fishing products exported.

Corn has always been produced in Belize, largely by the traditional *milpa* system of the Maya, using shifting slash-and-burn techniques and producing chiefly for the subsistence of the *milpero* and his family. Production of corn has increased substantially in the last two decades from 9 million pounds in 1964 to 23 million pounds in 1969, 34 million pounds in 1979, and 47 million pounds in 1982. When international corn prices fell in 1982, the Belize Marketing Board, a statutory body, effectively subsidized corn production by purchasing 4 million pounds of corn at $.24 a pound and selling them at $.15 a pound. The board also buys and sells rice and red kidney beans. The latter, another traditional crop, fell off in 1971, due to low prices received in the local market the previous year when over 5 million pounds were produced. Since 1978, however, the quantity of beans produced has increased steadily from 2.2 million pounds to 4 million in 1983. Beans are widely consumed throughout the Caribbean, so there is a potential for exporting this crop to CARICOM countries, such as Jamaica.

The potential for agricultural development in Belize remains enormous, and the gains made in recent years, dramatic as some of them have been, are merely a sign of what can be done. Only somewhere between 12 and 15 percent of the land suitable for agriculture is currently being farmed, and the government now has more than 1 million acres of good land, along with sound land tenure policies and a program

of agricultural credit, that make agricultural development the
country's top economic priority.

FISHING, TOURISM, LIGHT INDUSTRIES, AND SERVICES

Though agriculture has largely replaced forestry as the
basis of Belize's economy, other sectors also have been successfully developed in the past two decades. The development
of the fishing industry has been a success story: Five fishing
cooperatives, begun in the early 1960s, now catch, sort, clean,
freeze, and pack a variety of fish, including lobsters, shrimp,
conch, and red snapper, grouper, and other fish. The fishermen
are obliged by law to sell a proportion of their catch to the
local market at controlled prices, and regulations protect certain
species, such as lobster, from overfishing, but the enforcement
of such regulations is very difficult. Given the huge area of
good fishing waters in and near Belize, it would seem that
the fishing industry could be expanded, especially that involving scale fish, and shrimp farms could be developed. But
deep-sea fishing and fish farming are more expensive and
complicated operations that would require considerable expansion of the present industry—in investment, skilled per-
sonnel, and equipment. Until such developments, the volume
of fish exports is unlikely to increase much. The rapid increase
of the value of fish exports, from $3.6 million in 1978 to
$14.4 million in 1981, is chiefly the result of fishermen
concentrating on exporting the higher valued lobsters, which
accounted for about 90 percent of these earnings, but lobsters
are a distinctly limited resource. Despite problems and lim-
itations of resources, the fishing industry has been a useful
contributor to Belize's export earnings, especially in the years
when the value of sugar products declined. Between 1975
and 1983, the total value of fish products exported was $80
million, compared to $86.5 million for citrus products and
only $23 million for timber products. Fish products have
become the second most valuable domestic export, rising from
3 percent of the value of exports in 1978 to 11 percent in
1983.

The potential for tourism, like fishing, has not yet been developed in Belize. The country has great natural and cultural attractions, is conveniently close to the great North American market, and is safe for tourists. The coral reef and cayes offer the finest skin diving, underwater photography, sailing, and fishing in the hemisphere, along with the superlative sun, sea, and sand that visitors to the Caribbean take for granted. The nearest thing to a tourist development in Belize is at San Pedro on Ambergris Caye, an island at the north of the reef, bordering with Mexico. San Pedro's economy was based upon the plantation production of coconuts until the 1950s, and its people were little more than peons. Now the home of the successful Caribena fishing cooperative, registered in 1963, San Pedro has a good standard of living. The first hotel was opened on Ambergris Caye in 1965, and since then more than twenty hotels have made tourism an important part of the island's prosperity. Some fishermen put their savings into small family hotels that are very hospitable and comfortable. As North American investors have purchased ocean-front parcels for homes and hotels, or just speculation, land prices have recently soared out of reach of most Belizeans.

In addition to the longest reef in the hemisphere, with some 175 sandy cayes, Belize offers interesting inland sites for tourists, including some accessible Maya ruins (those of Altun Ha and Xunantunich receive 6,000 or 7,000 visitors a year), lofty waterfalls, huge caves, and varied tropical flora and fauna. Some 240 varieties of wild orchids and 500 species of birds are a nature lover's dream. Several tourist lodges and hotels offer safaris in the interior that combine natural and historical interests. At present, these tourist attractions are all small scale and have little negative social or environmental impact, and they do not tap the potential market very effectively. It is understandable that the government of Belize seeks to avoid some of the negative consequences of the mass tourist industry that have appeared elsewhere in the region, but at present Belize gets less than 1 percent of the North American tourist trade in the Caribbean. This share could be increased, to the benefit of existing hoteliers, if regional airlines provided a more reliable and cheaper service. Unfortunately, Belize Airways Ltd. was short lived, and then Air Florida collapsed. The remaining international carriers, from Honduras and El Salvador, cannot cope with present traffic and are frequently overbooked.

The number of Mexican visitors to Belize could increase, along with that of the Europeans who now visit Mexico, if regular airline services were established between those countries. Of 62,000 visitors to Belize in 1981, some 21,000 were from the United States, 22,000 from Central America (mostly migrant workers and refugees, rather than tourists), 6,000 from Mexico, 5,000 from Europe, and 2,000 each from Canada and Britain. When the runway of Belize International Airport was lengthened in 1968 to accommodate medium-sized planes, the passenger traffic increased, to 129,000 people in 1980 and 260,000 in 1982, thereby straining the airport facilities. The number of hotels has increased from 118 in 1979 to 150 in 1983, but, with occupancy rates as low as 35 percent in 1981 and 1982, the tourist industry is unlikely to expand unless there is a more comprehensive promotional program. A careful promotion and development of tourism along its present lines could contribute far more to the economy than at present while still avoiding negative side effects.

Belize has a few small light industries oriented chiefly toward the domestic market, for example, the production of flour, mattresses, cigarettes, beer and soft drinks, footwear, fertilizers, furniture, garments, batteries, and matches. In addition to the production of rum and citrus concentrates, a few small businesses now manufacture products like jams, jellies, and sauces from local agricultural produce. Some of these, of course, are more export oriented, including the fish processing plants, an animal feed plant, the rice mill, and the honey-producing industry. The garment industry of Belize is one of the largest light industries, but it uses imported materials so the local value added to these materials is quite low. (The value of garments exported fell from a peak $28.8 million in 1980 to $12.7 million in 1982, then rose to $16.8 million in 1983.)

The government has initiated a program of incentives to promote industrial development (the Development Incentives Laws of 1960, 1971, and 1973, the last dealing specifically with industrial enterprises), but manufacturing remains a minor sector of the Belizean economy and actually declined from 8.4 percent of the GDP in 1980 to 7.0 percent in 1982, whereas construction, the chief industrial activity for the domestic market, remained at around 5.7 percent. After a relatively rapid growth of largely import substitution industries in the 1970s, the manufacture of garments and cigarettes and the construction industry have fallen sharply since the recession of 1981 to 1982.

Services have become the largest segment of the economy since 1982, when they accounted for over 47 percent of the GDP, compared to 40 percent for agriculture, forestry, and fishing. Trade, administration, and tourism are the chief services, and, because of a 10 percent decline in trade and tourism in 1982, the combined service sector declined by an estimated 1 percent in that year. Many jobs in services are in the public sector, which includes the national government, which employs about 4,000 people (including temporary workers), nine statutory bodies (Water and Sewerage Authority, Belize Electricity Board, Telecommunications Authority, Belize Marketing Board, Belize Meats Ind., Banana Control Board, Port Authority, Social Security, and Reconstruction and Development Corporation and Housing), and two financial institutions (the Central Bank and the Development Finance Corporation). Health, education, and other social services provided by government and private and voluntary agencies employ many people at the national and community levels. The increasing importance of the services sector is reflected in the proportion of the labor force employed in it: an increase from about 28 percent in 1960 to 32 percent in 1980, whereas about one-third of the labor force remained in agriculture, forestry, and fishing, and the remainder in industry, transport, and other occupations. Although the occupations in the agricultural and industrial sectors remain largely male, three-quarters of the females employed were in the service sector in 1980, many in poorly paid domestic service and clerical work.

POWER, TRANSPORT, AND COMMUNICATIONS

Geological evidence suggests that good deposits of oil and gas may be present both onshore and offshore, but explorations, which began as long ago as 1938, have yet to bear fruit. Nine companies are now exploring various parts of the country, and forty wells have been drilled without discovering oil or gas in commercially viable quantities. The exploration licenses are said to be extremely liberal, allowing thirty years of exploitation if oil is found. Until such time, however, Belize is dependent on imported oil for its energy needs. (A new 75-kilowatt hydroelectric plant opened in 1983 at Blue Creek in Orange Walk District, but it supplies only the local villages.) More than half a million barrels of oil are imported per year; this amounted to 16 percent of total imports in 1981. The rise of crude oil prices from $6 to $64 per barrel between 1973 and 1980 drove up the cost of fuels imported into Belize from $2.8 million in 1970 to a staggering $54.5 million in 1980. The Belize Electricity Board, a statutory body, provides a notoriously unreliable supply of electricity to about 60 percent of the population. The government's plans to extend rural electrification will require additional production and a better transmission and distribution system. Rather than importing more fuel oils, Belize may in the future purchase bulk power from Mexico or develop its own renewable natural resources, including wood and sugarcane bagasse, and hydraulic, wind, and solar power.

Over half the consumption of oil is for transportation, a situation aggravated by the country's low population density in which relatively long distances separate scattered towns and villages. To the costs of transportation fuel are added the high per capita costs of constructing and maintaining a road network in sparsely populated districts. Belize has over 1,000 miles of improved roads, but only one-fourth of these are paved, as well as some 200 miles of tracks and 250 miles of urban streets. Poor road maintenance in many districts, combined with frequent flooding and flood damage, leads to unsatisfactory road transport conditions in many parts of the country.

All maritime imports are handled by Belize City's semi-deepwater port, but the port needs to be deepened from 17 to 32 feet to accommodate large oceangoing ships and bulk-sugar vessels. At present most agricultural exports are barged and transshipped, and a new deepwater port south of Belize City is badly needed to handle the export of sugar, bananas, and citrus products. The government has a plan for a new port at Big Creek that would reduce the present costs incurred in barging bananas to Honduras, but the project would cost at least $7 million.

The Belize International Airport is linked by domestic airlines and charter flights to the municipal airport at Belize City and eleven other government airstrips in all the districts. The international airport needs improvement, however, as the volume of traffic has increased, and plans have been made for an extension of the runway from 6,300 to 8,000 feet, for a new control tower with better navigational equipment, and for a new terminal building.

Belize's modern telephone system was established in the 1970s, and in 1979 the Belize Telecommunications Authority began expanding the number of lines by installing nine new exchanges. The number of subscribers increased from 3,800 in 1979 to 8,600 in 1983, and is projected to increase by about 1,000 annually for several years. Radio Belize provides the only broadcasting facilities. Founded in 1952, it has become a national institution, providing personal messages of deaths and emergencies for people in the more remote districts, as well as a variety of news, music, and entertainment programs, about a quarter of which are in Spanish. The growing use of television in the early 1980s has caused some problems of regulation. There is no Belizean television service, and a number of private operators are rebroadcasting satellite trans-missions to individual receivers. The fact that Belizeans now watch the programs of U.S. television stations, without having one of their own, is certain to increase greatly the cultural influence from that country. In July 1984, a law was passed to regulate radio and television broadcasting in Belize, in-cluding satellite broadcasting, to monitor its content, but the

Belize Broadcasting Authority is unlikely to halt the electronic cultural bombardment from the United States.

FINANCIAL INSTITUTIONS

The Monetary Authority, created in 1976, became the Central Bank of Belize in 1982. The act establishing the bank states that its chief objectives are to foster monetary stability, especially stability of the exchange rate, and economic growth. The bank inherited the functions of its predecessor, namely, managing the currency and foreign exchange reserves and performing banking services for the public sector, the commercial banks (of which there are four, all branches of foreign banks),[12] and other financial institutions. In addition to controls on liquidity and on the volume, terms, and conditions of credit, the Central Bank has the power to determine limits on domestic rates of interest. The bank is required to hold a reserve of external assets equal to not less than 40 percent of its currency in circulation and demand liabilities, and there are limits to the bank's holding of government treasury bills and other securities.[13]

The Development Finance Corporation (DFC), established in 1963, and owned by the government, has the goal of promoting long-term development funding and providing loans to small farmers, cooperatives, and businessmen who may not get credit from the commercial banks. The Caribbean Development Bank has been the chief source of funds, and agricultural and construction projects are the primary recipients of loans. The corporation's operations declined in 1982, in accord with the overall decline in economic activity in the recession. Nevertheless, the DFC has outstanding loans amounting to $24 million, or about 17 percent of Belize's financial system. About 3,000 loans have been approved for agriculture (41 percent of the total), housing (30 percent), tourism (8 percent), manufacturing (7 percent), fishing (4 percent), and various services (10 percent). The DFC also holds equity amounting to $2.2 million in five companies, one of which is the DFC Investment Company, designed to invest directly in economic activities.

Belize's credit union system, started in the 1940s, is well established and operates throughout the country. In 1983, thirty-eight credit unions were active, rivaling in many ways the commercial banks. The elected credit committees of the credit unions supervise loans to their members. The Holy Redeemer Credit Union is the largest, with some 20,000 members and $13 million of assets in 1982, a year when it issued loans worth $3.3 million, chiefly for home building and improvement, business and industry, vehicles, home appliances and furniture, and education.

The Central Bank, despite its legal authority, has only a very limited ability to influence economic activity because of the extreme dependence of Belize's economic system on the world economy. The Central Bank was able to persuade the commercial banks to reduce local interest rates in 1983, after several years in which the prime rate had risen from 9 to 17 percent, really only because international interest rates had begun to decline. On the small scale of the credit unions, Belizeans can learn the principles and practice of financial management, but the Central Bank is so tied to international monetary policies that it can hardly live up to its role as an agent for transforming and developing the national economy. Insurance companies remain outside the Central Bank's influence, and the commercial banks are controlled by the transnational companies of which they are minor branches. Rather than overseeing the financial system, the Central Bank is often relegated merely to observing and responding to it.

LABOR AND UNEMPLOYMENT

In 1946 the labor force recorded in the census numbered 20,133, or about 55 percent of the population over 15 years of age. The economically active population has increased rapidly, to 27,000 people in 1960, 33,000 in 1970, and over 46,000 in 1980. As a percentage of the population over 15 years old, this labor force has increased to 58 percent in 1960, 60 percent in 1970, and 65 percent in 1980. The increase in female participation has been most dramatic, from 20.6

percent in 1960 to 30.3 percent in 1980, whereas the proportion of males in the labor force has remained at about 98 percent. The increase in labor force participation during the last four decades, from 55 to 65 percent, has largely resulted from the rapid rise in the number of economically active women.

The proportion of the labor force engaged in agriculture, forestry, and fishing has fallen during this century from about 47 percent before World War II, to about 40 percent in the 1940s and 1950s, to about a third of the labor force in 1970 and 1980. This sector remains by far the largest, employing some 40 percent of the male labor force. The next largest sector is industry and transport, with about 24 percent of the labor force and again employing a higher proportion of men. Over three-quarters of the women employed are in the professional and technical, clerical, sales, and service sectors, which together employ a total of 31.5 percent of the labor force.

Gross national product (GNP) per capita is around $2,000 and appears to be relatively evenly distributed in comparison with countries like Guatemala and Jamaica, but income distribution figures are not available. The average annual income of paid employees, who constitute about two-thirds of the labor force, is estimated to be $6,000. No general minimum wage is legislated in Belize, but legal minimum wages are established for domestic service in private homes ($1.10 per hour), in hotels ($1.25 per hour), and places where alcoholic beverages are sold ($1.50 per hour). Actual wages for most unskilled workers vary between $1.15 and $1.35 per hour for women and $1.40 and $1.70 per hour for men. Women generally earn lower wages than men, often a quarter or a third lower, even when they do exactly the same work. Any overtime in excess of nine hours per day or forty-eight hours per week must be given an additional 50 percent payment, and the minimum paid vacation is six working days per year. Maternity leave consists of six weeks before and after childbirth, by law, and sixteen sick leave days are allotted per year, the first three to be paid in full by social security, the next thirteen by the employer. Labor legislation also specifies minimum conditions of payment and notice of termination of employment, depending on the length of time the person has been employed.

Unemployment statistics are notoriously hard to find and unreliable. However, unemployment, which has increased in recent years, is an acute problem in some areas, such as Belize City where the unemployment rate was estimated at 22 percent in 1980 *before* the recent recession. In fact, about half of the unemployed workers of Belize, officially 14.3 percent of the labor force in 1980, were in Belize City. The fact that 68 percent of the unemployed were in the age range of fifteen to nineteen years suggests that employment prospects were generally good for older workers: Less than 5 percent of the labor force were unemployed workers of twenty years or more in 1980, according to the census. The unemployment rate was highest (54 percent) among young women, aged fifteen to nineteen years. Unemployment is increasing as hundreds of people were laid off by Belize Sugar Industries in 1985. Moreover, underemployment is widespread: Only about two-thirds of the people counted as employed actually work full time.

If the participation of women in the labor force continues to increase and migration abroad continues at the rate of about 1 percent of the population per year, the labor force will grow, as it did in the 1970s, at about 3.4 percent per year. To absorb the new workers entering the labor force, the economy would have to grow more than 6 percent a year. However, the annual growth rate, which had averaged about 5 percent between 1978 and 1981, fell to almost zero after 1981 because of the sugar crisis and other problems associated with the international recession. Moreover, expansion of the economy is most likely to occur in agriculture and hence will not provide jobs for the urban youth and women who constitute so great a part of the unemployed. The long-term decline in the proportion of the labor force employed in agriculture, forestry, and fishing—from about one-half in 1931 to one-third today—and the spread of an urban consumer lifestyle, as promoted by the trade, travel, and television contacts with U.S. culture, do not make agricultural labor attractive to young Belizeans. Young people in Belize City would rather emigrate than participate as seasonal wage earners in the sugar and citrus industries or as small farmers in rural areas. As a result, some 1,500 migrant workers come to Belize from neighboring countries every year to work in the sugar and citrus areas during crop season, and the government is willing to settle immigrants, whether refugees or others interested in agriculture, on easy terms. If neither a rapid change in the attitudes of urban Belizeans nor a rapid growth in the economy takes place, it is easy to predict an increase in unemployment in Belize in the 1980s.

ECONOMIC DEVELOPMENT

The Belizean economy is similar in many respects to those of other small developing countries. The economy is predominantly agricultural, with a very unequal distribution and low utilization of agricultural land and a heavy reliance upon the export of a narrow range of agricultural products. Ownership of the economy is chiefly in the private sector with foreign investment dominating the important sectors of banking, insurance, manufacturing, and sugarcane processing. A high population growth rate and increasing unemployment are coupled with a chronic trade gap resulting from continuing dependence upon imports of food, fuels, and manufactured goods. The economic infrastructure is often inadequate and poorly maintained, as in the roads, port facilities, and electricity production. Like most other small countries in the region, Belize has suffered from the recession of 1982–1983, especially the sugar crisis, because of its continuing dependence on the U.S. and British economies.

To balance these negative points, many positive aspects can be seen in the Belizean economy. Within three decades, the economy has been transformed from one entirely dependent upon the moribund forestry industry to an expanding and fairly diversified agricultural economy. The historical dominance of absentee landlords with their narrow forest interests has been broken, and, because the government owns large tracts of mostly unutilized land, further agricultural development is possible, if people with the skills and capital are available to seize the opportunity. Though private, foreign ownership of the economy remains widespread, significant shifts have occurred in recent years, even in the chief industries of sugar, citrus, and fishing, as well as in small farming, apiculture, and tourism, that show that Belizeans, as individuals and in cooperatives, with or without government help, are developing and managing important areas of their economy. Though the natural population increase remains high and several thousand refugees have settled in Belize in the last few years, this is balanced by large-scale emigration, so the population growth rate has fallen from over 3 percent in the 1950s to less than 2 percent in the 1970s. Given the prolific agricultural and fishing potential of Belize, such a growth rate is not excessive and unemployment could be reduced if people could be persuaded of the benefits of a productive rural life. If we bear in mind the complete neglect during three centuries of colonialism, then the extension of roads, the new airport and port facilities, the construction of the new capital, and the electrification of rural areas that have taken place in the past two decades are quite impressive.

The economy expanded steadily during the 1960s and most of the 1970s, when the GDP grew at 4 to 5 percent per year. Sugar production accounts to a large extent for this performance as it amounts to about a quarter of the GDP. The value of sugar exported doubled from about $10 million in the late 1960s to $20 million in 1973, after the new factory at Tower Hill began operation. Since then, the vicissitudes of sugar prices, down in 1976 and 1979 and again in 1981 and 1982, have been reflected in the economy at large, but Belize appears to have weathered these crises and to have emerged in better shape financially than most other countries in the region. Belize has tried to compensate for the recent drastic fall in sugar prices by increasing production, but 90,424 tons of sugar exported in 1981 were valued at $85 million whereas 96,750 tons exported in 1985 were estimated to be worth only $50 million. Belize was able to cope with these uncertainties and crises in sugar production and prices because nonsugar agriculture and manufacturing have performed satisfactorily since 1978. In particular, the increased production of fish products, citrus products, rice, red kidney beans, bananas, poultry, and honey have diversified the economy and earned foreign exchange while making Belize more self-sufficient in food. So local developments have been promising, despite the worsening sugar crisis, the 4.5 percent decline in real gross domestic income, and increasing unemployment since 1982, which resulted chiefly from the impact of the international recession.

The government's stated policy is to promote "economic development and social progress by means of a mixed economy in which the public sector works in partnership with the private sector for increased production, balanced development and social well-being. . . . The public sector engages in direct productive and other economic activities only where necessary, and will do so in partnership in private enterprise where possible."[14] In seeking to promote a climate attractive to both local and foreign investors, the government seems to be drawn increasingly to active involvement and participation in the economy. In addition to providing the basic infrastructure and manpower training, the government attempts to exercise greater control over the financial system and economic growth through the Central Bank and over investment and development through the Development Finance Corporation and the DFC Investment Company. Through its ownership of large tracts of land and its recent involvement with Belize Sugar Industries, the government may expand its economic activities, as much by necessity as by policy. Public-sector activities now represent about 30 percent of GDP, in production (for example, of bananas) as well as traditional services (water, electricity, ports, roads, sewerage, communications, social security, health, and education). Public investments, representing 60 to 70 percent of the total domestic investment and about 15 percent of GDP, have played an important role in Belize's development. The financing of these investments, as well as the technical assistance, is increasingly supplied by external donors and lenders, and the government is responsible for developing these projects. In 1975, external capital funded 27 percent of the total public investment, and by 1982–1983 this figure had risen to over 70 percent. The new government, elected in 1984, has criticized the private banks for making an insufficient contribution to national development. Despite its more conservative ideology this government must continue to promote development.

The former government accorded top priority in its development strategy to projects that develop agriculture and livestock production and agroindustries, and it encouraged foreign investment in these areas. According to the Belize Investment Code, such investment is welcome if it uses local raw materials, produces for export, and contributes to the employment and upgrading of Belizeans' skills. Preference is given to joint ventures in which local entrepreneurs participate, "in keeping with Government's policy of insuring the maximum participation by Belizeans in the enjoyment of our natural resource endowments."[15] The government is trying to reassure potential foreign investors who may be deterred by the political and military situation in the region and by the still unresolved Guatemalan claim. Although recognizing the need for a mixed economy and for a large share for the public sector, the government does not want to alienate local businessmen, foreign investors, or foreign sources of aid. In 1984, Minister of Economic Development Said Musa pushed the opportunities for investment and trade in Britain, Japan, Taiwan, Hong Kong, and the United States, at the same time as he expressed hope for more economic cooperation between the nations of the region.

Belize joins members of the Non-Aligned movement in seeking major reforms in the international economic order. Because Belize has a small economy that relies heavily on imports and upon the export of a few products for its income, it is vulnerable to sudden drops in export values or increases in fuel prices and dependent upon trade with the United States and Britain. Over the past two decades, the government has been trying, often in very adverse circumstances, to promote a more self-reliant and autonomous economy, and part of that effort has been directed through association with other former British colonies in the Caribbean. In 1971, Belize joined the Caribbean Free Trade Association (CARIFTA), which became the Caribbean Community (CARICOM) in 1973.

Accorded less-developed-country status, Belize is developing its trade with the member nations. Exports to CARICOM amounted to only 3.4 percent of total exports in 1975 and 1978 and about 4 percent in 1980 and 1981, but rose to 14 percent in 1983. Like the changes in production in recent decades, this increase shows a promising diversification in the direction of trade exports. Regional economic cooperation is not a panacea, but it may help reduce the extreme dependence of such small economies on the metropolitan giants.

Because Belize is so small and its economy is so open, it is largely dependent on the international situation. Despite the successful expansion and diversification of the economy in the 1960s and 1970s, the Belizean economy suffered from the international recession of 1982–1983, and its recovery depends upon a recovery of the world economy. With abundant natural resources and essentially sound government policies, the prospects for Belize's economic development in the next decade or two look good, provided the international recovery takes place. The external public debt has been increasing rapidly in recent years, and debt services will increase as soon as several loans, including those the government incurred in response to the 1981–1982 financial difficulties, become repayable. If the anticipated recovery does not take place and the Belize economy grows at less than about 5 percent a year, it may be headed for the familiar downward spiral associated with emergency IMF assistance and all the human hardship, social disruption, and political instability that come in its train. Belize clearly has the means to develop, but it remains to be seen whether it will get the chance.

NOTES

1. N. S. Carey Jones, *The Pattern of a Dependent Economy: The National Income of British Honduras* (Cambridge, Cambridge University Press, 1953), p. 18.

2. *Latin American Weekly Report*, 29 June 1984, p. 4.

3. See O. Nigel Bolland, "Systems of Domination after Slavery: The Control of Land and Labor in the British West Indies after 1838," *Comparative Studies in Society and History* (*CSSH*) 23, no.

4 (1981), and the subsequent debate, including William A. Green, "The Perils of Comparative History: Belize and the British Sugar Colonies after Slavery," and Bolland's reply, *CSSH* 26, no. 1 (1984):112–125.

4. 28 February 1967, BA, R 96; see O. Nigel Bolland, "The Maya and the Colonization of Belize in the Nineteenth Century," in *Anthropology and History in Yucatán*, Grant D. Jones, ed. (Austin, University of Texas Press, 1977), pp. 69–99.

5. In 1787, Superintendent Despard listed a Hoare as one of the chief Baymen who held mahogany works in an "illegal manner," 31 October 1787, CO 123/6.

6. Oliver V. G. Hoare to Sir Samuel H. Wilson, 24 September 1931, CO 123/335.

7. Kathleen M. Stahl, *The Metropolitan Organization of British Colonial Trade* (London, Faber and Faber, 1951), p. 31.

8. "A Development Plan for British Honduras, Part Two— The Modernization of Agriculture" (United Nations, 1963).

9. A. A. Hunter, *Rural Land Utilization Tax* (Belize City, n.d.), p. 8.

10. See O. Nigel Bolland and Assad Shoman, *Land in Belize, 1765–1871* (Kingston, Institute of Social and Economic Research, 1977), pp. 112–14.

11. This company had been seeking to sell large portions of its land, in lots of over 5,000 acres, mostly to U.S. speculators because few Belizeans could afford the price. Belize Estate and Produce Company, reduced to 709,000 acres mostly in western Orange Walk but including valuable property in Belize City and agencies for Ford vehicles and Johnny Walker scotch, was bought by William F. Belote of the United States in 1980, who sold it in 1983 to Barry M. Bowen, a member of a wealthy Belize business family. The Bowen empire, which includes the Coca Cola franchise, the Belize Brewing Co., varied importing agencies, majority shares in the country's largest retail store, and an aerial crop dusting service, was worth US$23 million in 1982. With the purchase of the Belize Estate and Produce Company and the attempt to form Hillbank Agroindustry Ltd., Bowen may have overextended his resources. His proposal for a wood-burning power station could be ecologically disastrous for Belize.

12. A Bank of British Honduras, founded by local financiers in 1904, was bought by the Royal Bank of Canada in 1912. The Royal Bank issued private notes until 1937, when the Currency Commission took over the function of providing currency. The four

commercial banks in Belize today are the Royal Bank, Barclay's, the Bank of Nova Scotia, and Atlantic Bank.

13. Central Bank of Belize, *First Annual Report and Accounts* (1982), p. 4.

14. *Belize Investment Code* (Belize, n.d.), pp. 1–2.

15. *Belize Investment Code*, p. 2.

Update, October 1985: Two very recent developments in the sugar and citrus industries indicate a major turn in Belize's economy in the next decade. First, Tate and Lyle has now negotiated its withdrawal by placing 82 percent of the shares of BSI into a trust on behalf of the Tower Hill factory employees. The British multinational retains a 10 percent shareholding and any dividends that may be declared until 1994. As production and the U.S. quota for 1985–1986 will be much reduced, it seems the new owners have acquired a liability. Second, Minute Maid, a subsidiary of Coca Cola, has purchased a 30 percent share in about 600,000 acres of Bowen's Hillbank estate in Orange Walk district (part of the Belize Estate and Produce Company). It is expected to clear 25,000 acres of forest as part of a planned U.S. $120 million investment in huge orange plantations and a processing plant. These two developments point to a change from sugar to citrus as Belize's chief export crop and from British to United States control of the economy.

5

Politics and External Relations

THE COLONIAL RELATIONSHIP

The colonial relationship between Belize and Britain was a peculiar one. For so long just a small settlement of wood-cutters and their slaves, Belize was neglected almost completely by Britain in the eighteenth century. The sugar islands were far more valuable, and Britain was reluctant to offend Spain by too openly encouraging the colonists. British assertion of sovereignty over Belize came piecemeal in the nineteenth century with a declaration in 1817 that the Crown should be the sole authority for granting titles to land; with the assumption by the superintendent in 1832 of the power to appoint magistrates; with the adoption of a formal constitution in 1854 and the regularization of the legal system the following year; with the declaration in 1862 that it was a colony called British Honduras; with the change to Crown colony status in 1871; and, finally, with the termination of the colony's official dependence on Jamaica in 1884. This last feature, which had been imposed since 1841 when the superintendent was ordered to send all his dispatches through the governor of Jamaica, indicated that in the imperial scheme Belize was a second-class colony. With the expansion of the British Empire in Asia and Africa and the decline of the West Indian sugar interest in the nineteenth century, British officials paid little attention to the poor frontier colony in Central America.

Until 1936, Belize was governed by the governor-in-council, the council being entirely nominated by the governor, initially with a majority of official over unofficial members.

When a request was made in 1890 to reintroduce elected members, as was the case in the largely white colonies of Canada and New Zealand, it was turned down on the grounds that only about 400 people in a population of over 30,000 were white. An unofficial majority was instituted in 1892, but since the unofficial members were still chosen by the governor, this change was not major. Further agitation for a return to the elective principle in the 1920s was viewed favorably by the Colonial Office, provided there was a return to an official majority or the governor was given reserve powers to push through any measures he considered essential, with or without council consent. The council rejected these provisos, and the issue of restoring elections was dropped. After the terrible hurricane of 1931, the council was forced to accept the granting of reserve powers for the governor as a condition for the British government's raising a reconstruction loan. Battered by the depression and the hurricane, Belize took a step backward when the imperial government strengthened its control over the increasingly dependent colony.

In the nineteenth century, the Crown colony system was the constitutional means by which the British government exercised its administrative control in the West Indian colonies over the vested interests and working people alike. Generally, however, the vested interests had been so co-opted into the system—as unofficial members of the Legislative Council—that they came to see the Crown colony regime as a defense against the rising democratic agitation of the majority. From the middle of the nineteenth century in the West Indies, according to political scientist Gordon Lewis, "fear of the Negro masses . . . combined with a conviction that they could never look after themselves, lay at the heart of British policy. That combination of class and colour phobias dominated the official outlook for the next one hundred years."[1] Yet within the past half-century, quicker in some places and slower in others, the British colonies of the Caribbean, including Belize, have developed from Crown colony status through self-government to full independence. The spark that set the independence movements aflame was the working-class agitation begun in the 1930s, and one of the first places where this occurred was Belize.

Within the prevailing stagnation that had characterized Belizean economy and society for most of the century prior to the 1930s, the seeds of change were discernible. The chronic depression in the mahogany trade, the emergence of the chicle business, and several attempts to develop the plantation cultivation of various crops were followed by technological innovations in timber extraction and then the catastrophic depression of the 1930s. Trade, meanwhile, had shifted increasingly from Britain to the United States, and this fact, combined with the predominance of U.S. Catholic teachers in Belizean schools, began to erode the traditional colonial ties and gave rise to a U.S.-oriented commercial elite. While this emerging Creole middle class was dissatisfied with the close connections between the colonial administration and the old British businesses, the working people were increasingly dissatisfied with the injustices of the colonial system, as evidenced in the riots of 1919, and the sheer poverty and near starvation that followed the depression and hurricane.

What developed in 1934 and 1935, with Antonio Soberanis' Labourers and Unemployed Association (LUA), was a growing working-class consciousness and an incipient nationalism, often growing together. In a petition to the governor on 17 May 1934, Soberanis declared that "we are a new People . . . the People of British Honduras should raise the cry of British Honduras for British Hondurans. . . . British Honduras has been sleeping for over a Century, not dead, only sleeping. . . . Today British Honduras is walking around."[2] As president of the British Honduras Workers and Tradesmen Union in 1941, Soberanis stated that "trade Unionism is a very great thing, its [sic] the only medium by which the working class can get a square deal."[3] In 1940, several people, some of whom had been in the LUA, formed a British Honduras Independent Labour party, later called the People's Republican party, advocating a local republic with the name Belize Honduras. The nationalists were attacked by loyalists waving the Union Jack, and their leaders, Joseph Campbell, Gabriel Adderley, and John Lahoodie, were imprisoned.[4] The following year, mass meetings were held throughout the colony, in which adult suffrage and the right to elect the government were demanded.[5]

This persistent agitation won several concessions on the industrial and political fronts. The legalization of trade unions, the removal of labor contracts from the jurisdiction of the criminal code, and other reforms in labor legislation ushered in a new era of labor relations in the 1940s. The political and constitutional concessions were also introduced piecemeal, beginning with a return to the elective principle in the constitution of 1936. Having passed new laws in 1935 that gave police the power to ban processions, redefined sedition (Soberanis was detained under this law from November 1935 to February 1936), and gave the governor extra powers in an emergency, like a riot, the colonial administration felt confident enough to allow five of the thirteen members of the Legislative Council to be elected, albeit on a highly restricted franchise. A combination of property or income and literacy qualifications restricted the electorate to 1,035 in a population of about 56,000. The governor retained his reserve powers to ensure that the Colonial Office would have its way on any major issues. Between 1939 and 1954 six members in a Legislative Council of fourteen members were elected by a tiny minority— between 1 and 2 percent of the population. In 1945, for instance, 822 voters were registered in a population of over 63,000. The proportion of voters increased slightly in 1950, partly because the minimum age for women voters was reduced from thirty to twenty-one years and partly because the devaluation of the dollar effectively reduced the property and income qualifications.

Not until 1954 did Belize achieve universal adult suffrage under a constitution that created a Legislative Assembly consisting of nine elected members, three nominated unofficial members, and three official members. The governor still had reserve powers, and elected members were a minority in the Executive Council (four out of ten members), but the struggle for democracy and self-government had clearly begun to tip in favor of the Belizean people. The governor no longer sat in the legislature, which was presided over by a speaker, but he remained very much the chief executive. The biggest change lay in the introduction of adult suffrage, which revolutionized the political life of the country. For twenty years the working people of Belize had participated in politics without candidates or a party of their own and without having the vote. The 1954 constitution finally authorized what had increasingly been a reality—the mass participation of Belizeans in their own political affairs. Crown colony government was gone, and it seemed that colonialism itself would soon follow; yet independence was delayed until 1981.

Before describing the independence movement and the chief reasons for the delayed decolonization, I will outline the modern constitutional history of Belize as it reflects a changing relationship with Britain. The constitutional history from 1936 to 1985 may be divided into five periods. During the first period, from 1936 to 1954, the elected members of the Legislative Council were in a minority and were elected by a tiny minority of the population. The second period commenced with the adoption of the 1954 constitution, which created a Legislative Assembly containing a majority of members elected by a majority of the people, but executive power remained with the governor. The third period, from 1960 to 1963, saw a continuation of the advance toward self-government. The Legislative Assembly was expanded from fifteen to twenty-five members, eighteen of whom were elected, and a majority of the Executive Council were elected members. The governor remained on the council as chairman but without a vote.

The fourth period began in 1964 and culminated in independence in 1981. Full internal self-government was provided by a constitution that created a bicameral legislature, the National Assembly, consisting of a House of Representatives of eighteen elected members and a Senate of eight nominated members. After a general election, the governor, as a symbolic representative of the Queen, appointed as premier the member of the House of Representatives who was best able to command majority support. The premier then appointed his cabinet, the chief policymaking body, which was collectively responsible to the National Assembly.

Between 1964 and 1981, the British government retained authority through the governor over foreign affairs, defense, internal security, and the terms and conditions of appointment of the civil service, leaving all other matters to the premier and his cabinet. Finally, on 21 September 1981, Belize became a fully independent member of the Commonwealth of Nations, meaning that, although the Queen of England remains the head of state, represented by the governor-general, her function is ceremonial. All authority now resides in the government of Belize, led by the prime minister, and Belize is a sovereign nation. In this fifth period, the number of elected representatives has been increased to twenty-eight.

The decolonization of the British territories in the Caribbean was an evolutionary and, in most instances, a relatively orderly affair. Since the Wood Report of 1922, the British government had accepted the principle that constitutional advancement should take place toward some form of representative government, but the pace of change advocated by the British was more leisurely than that desired by the awakening people of the colonies. The British initially sought to keep the elected members a minority in order to retain official control and to keep the franchise narrow to neutralize the more radical political elements. The "class and colour phobias" to which Lewis refers were still strong, and the liberalization of British policy only went far enough to enable the mostly colored representatives of the middle classes—those who were more educated in British ways and had a considerable stake in stability—to participate in the colonial system. The British felt that a small group of privileged electors and elected legislators would tend to identify with the power elite and would seek to protect their political monopoly in the face of more radical, democratic demands. But the twentieth century was not like the nineteenth century, and democracy was a more likely alternative to autocratic Crown colony regimes than a return to some form of oligarchy. The labor rebellion of the 1930s provided the necessary impetus toward more representative government. Universal adult suffrage was achieved by Belize a decade after Jamaica, and it was linked in Belize, as elsewhere, to the establishment of an elected majority in the legislature.

By 1954, the independence movement in Belize was well organized so the achievement of representative government was followed by the demand that the elected members play a greater role in policymaking. The British government initially conceded to this demand by allowing the governor to appoint some of the elected members to the Executive Council, though these remained a minority until 1960. The next step in this leisurely constitutional decolonization was to feature a majority of elected members in the Executive Council, who then gained more power over the initiation of policy. As quasi ministers, these people had no real authority, but the British government's strategy gave them administrative experience. In this tutelary system, conceived as a transition to internal self-government, the elected members had a certain amount of responsibility but no real power. In the final preindependence phase, beginning in Belize in 1964, the Executive Council evolved from the governor's advisory body to a cabinet of ministers presided over by the premier and responsible for initiating public policy regarding almost all internal affairs.

In 1961, Ian Macleod, then British secretary of state for the colonies, stated that Belize could become constitutionally independent whenever it desired. The fact that Belize's independence was delayed for another twenty years resulted, not from British intransigence, but from the threat of recolonization by Guatemala. By the early 1960s, when Jamaica and Trinidad and Tobago (in 1962) and Barbados and Guyana (in 1966) were becoming independent, Britain was confident that Belize too was ready for independence. Such readiness was defined in terms of internal and external affairs: Internally, it meant that Belize had become accustomed to the form of parliamentary democracy known as the Westminster-Whitehall model, had adopted basic human rights and freedoms in its constitution, including the protection of property, and a legal system based upon the British one; and externally, it meant that Belize was expected to maintain its traditional allegiances and trade connections in international and economic affairs.

To the extent that these commercial ties and economic controls, as well as cultural and political influences, result in strategic limits, accommodations, and compromises in Belize's public policies, they are an effective brake upon the exercise of sovereign power. The persistence of such neocolonial restraints was a goal of Britain's evolutionary and tutelary decolonization policy, and it is an inevitable consequence of the inheritance of colonial institutions, systems, and processes, especially for very small states. In Belize, however, the problem of trying to eliminate all traces of residual colonialism is exacerbated by its continued dependence upon British forces for defense against Guatemala. Though Britain no doubt wants to withdraw its armed forces, which cost an estimated US$50 million annually, Belize's continued reliance upon them suggests an extraordinary constraint upon its independence.

Doubtless some ultraconservative colonial loyalists are still present in Belize, chiefly among the middle-class Creoles, but as the mother country shifted her attention from the residual empire and commonwealth toward the European Common Market in the 1960s, such people had little reason to hope for continuing colonial ties. The British strategy had begun with an attempt to create a federation of the West Indies after World War II, thereby disposing of its smaller colonies by joining them in a regional group. Belizean representatives decisively rejected the federal experiment in 1957, and the federation collapsed in 1961. These events left Belizeans with a fairly clear alternative: either recolonization by Guatemala or independence. Most Belizeans are not well-informed about Guatemala, but what they do know they do not like, and they certainly do not want to become Guatemala's twenty-third department, as Belice is defined in Guatemala's 1945 constitution. When independence finally came to Belize, it was greeted with enthusiasm by most Belizeans. There were still some basic Anglophiles, of course, such as those who hark back to the battle of St. George's Cay in 1798 as a famous English victory over the scheming Spaniards, but the vast majority were eager to cut the final colonial ties and to get on with their new, independent life. Whatever reservations some Belizeans may still have stem from their realistic concerns about their fragile country's ability to chart an independent course amid worldwide economic recession and regional wars. Although not underestimating the cultural and economic legacies of colonialism, few people in Belize today have any sentimental attachment to Britain, and, one may assume, none of these is in the younger half of the population.

POLITICAL PARTIES AND PERSONALITIES

For thirty-five years, politics in Belize has been dominated by one person, George Cadle Price. Middle class by family background and education, George Price first considered a career in the Catholic Church. He graduated from the elite secondary school, St. John's College, and then studied with the Jesuits in the United States in the 1930s. When he returned to Belize in 1942, instead of entering the priesthood he became secretary for Robert Turton, the Creole chicle millionaire who was an elected member of the Legislative Council between 1936 and 1948. Price entered politics through the Belize City Council. He failed to get elected in 1943 but succeeded in 1947, a year that began with a successful General Workers Union (GWU) strike at the Belize Estate and Produce Company's sawmill in Belize City.

At least three strands can be seen in Belizean politics in the 1940s. One, originating with Soberanis' Labourers and Unemployed Association (LUA) (1934–1937) and continuing through the British Honduras Workers and Tradesmen Union and the British Honduras Federation of Workers Protection Association (both organized in 1939) to the GWU, was working class in nature and emphasized labor issues. The second, a radical nationalist movement, emerged during the war. Its leaders came from the LUA and the local branch of Marcus Garvey's Universal Negro Improvement Association. It called itself variously the British Honduras Independent Labour party, the People's Republican party, and the People's National Committee. The third strand consisted of those who engaged in electoral politics within the narrow limits defined by the constitution and whose goals included the "Natives First" campaign and an extension of the franchise to elect more

George Cadle Price, prime minister 1964–1984

representative government. This last strand included professional people like the black lawyer, Arthur Balderamos, who supported labor but not adult suffrage, as well as the white and Creole merchants and employers who were out to defend their business interests. Turton, for all his antigovernment rhetoric, appeared largely indifferent to the distress of the working people and was really furthering his own interests, which were those of the rising Creole middle and upper classes. Price's political origins lay among the businessmen and merchants, the Creole middle and upper classes, who dominated politics within the Belize City Council, and the elected members of the Legislative Council after 1936. But Price, unlike most others, was able to broaden his political base by appealing to the labor and nationalist strands of Belizean politics at an early stage of his career.

Price was one of the group of young St. John's College graduates who won control of the Belize City Council in 1947 and started a newspaper, the *Belize Billboard*, to present their critiques of colonial policies. The U.S. connections of many of this group were evident when, at a rally on 10 September 1948 organized to counter the traditional loyalists' commemoration of the battle of St. George's Cay, they sang the "Stars and Stripes" and "God Bless America." This pro-U.S. element has been persistent: Turton's fortune originated in trade with Wrigley's of Chicago, and the radical nationalists advocated some kind of union with the United States in 1940.[6] Although these politicians and the *Billboard* drew attention to the plight of poor working people, they kept their distance from Clifford Betson, the more radical president of the GWU. When Betson called for the introduction of socialism into Belize in his New Year's message in 1948, the *Billboard* editors, Leigh Richardson, a former teacher, and Philip Goldson, a former civil servant, dissociated themselves, calling the message a "dangerous tendency." Socialism, they claimed, was the enemy of "individual progress and national unity."[7] Price's middle-class political associates were antisocialist as well as anticolonial and pro free-enterprise capitalism as well as pro-American.

When Price topped the polls in the 1947 election he opposed immigration and import controls and rode a wave of feeling against the British-proposed West Indian Federation. From the start, he was an eclectic and pragmatic politician, and one who often obscured his real ideological position under the cloak of religious values and quotations. Despite his limited political background, Price's skill as a politician quickly became apparent and enabled him to maintain his preeminent position for longer than any other national leader in the entire region. He was secretary of the People's United party before Castro's attack on the Moncada Barracks and before Eric Williams launched the People's National movement in Trinidad. His opponents and supporters alike agree that Price is an extraordinarily skillful politician, and, now in his midsixties, he is very experienced.

The event that precipitated the formation of the People's United party (PUP) and George Price's career was the devaluation of the British Honduras dollar on 31 December 1949. The several strands of Belizean politics came together because the devaluation provided an opportunity for various labor and nationalist forces to rally around a clear issue. First, devaluation was effected by the governor, using his reserve powers, in defiance of the Legislative Council and after repeated assurances by the British government since the devaluation of sterling in September, that the dollar would not be devalued. This action, then, exposed the limits of the existing representative system of administration and the extent of the colonial government's power over Belize. Their inferior colonial status was an aggravating insult to the educated middle classes who were eager for a more representative and responsible form of government. Second, the devaluation led to an immediate and easily calculable fall in the purchasing power of the people, while it protected the interests of the big transnationals like the Belize Estate and Produce Company, whose trade with the sterling area would be at a disadvantage without devaluation. The working people of Belize, subjected to widespread unemployment and poverty, were the chief sufferers as devaluation resulted in a rise in the price of imported U.S. goods, including food. This then, was a clear issue to unite labor, nationalists, and Creole middle classes in opposition to the governor and the colonial administration. On the very night that devaluation was declared, the People's Committee was formed and the independence movement was born.[8]

Between 1950 and 1954, the People's United party, formed upon the dissolution of the People's Committee on 29 September 1950, consolidated its organization, established its popular base, and articulated its primary demands. The agitation of individuals and organizations since the 1930s played an important part in all of these, and significant connections can be seen. For example, the *Billboard*, started as a weekly in 1947, became a daily paper in 1950 and gave its full support, with strongly anticolonial editorials, to the PUP. One of the original editors, Philip Goldson, was a prominent member of the People's Committee and became assistant secretary of the PUP, and the paper became in effect the official party organ. Most important, however, was the strong support from the GWU, whose president, Clifford Betson, was one of the original members of the People's Committee. Without the support of the GWU, the only extant mass organization of the working people of Belize, the early success of the PUP would have been unthinkable. Before the end of January 1950, the People's Committee and the GWU were holding joint meetings, discussing issues ranging from devaluation to labor legislation and from federation to constitutional reform. On 28 April, however, the middle-class members of the People's Committee took over the leadership of the union. Nicholas Pollard became president, John Smith, vice-president, and Price and Goldson, members of the Executive Council. All these men had been members of the Christian Social Action group in the 1940s, working with other St. John's College alumni to promote Catholic ideas on social justice. Betson fought this takeover, but, after seven years as a militant and pioneering union chief, he was given the dubious honorific title of "Patriarch of the Union." The political leaders took control of the union to use its strength, but the union movement declined as it became increasingly dependent upon the politicians in the 1950s. The provisional leaders of the PUP named in October 1950 were John Smith, party leader; Leigh Richardson, chairman; George Price, secretary; and Philip Goldson, assistant secretary. Five of the party's six candidates were elected to the Belize City Council in November 1950, winning 49 percent of the vote despite the restricted franchise, and the PUP tightened its hold on the GWU at the union's annual convention in April 1951. The two organizations became virtually identical, as Pollard was reelected president, Price became vice-president, Goldson and Richardson became, respectively, assistant secretary and corresponding secretary, and Smith became an executive councillor. Two days later the first PUP convention confirmed these men as party leaders.

During the subsequent months the PUP concentrated on agitating for constitutional reforms, including universal adult suffrage without a literacy test, an all-elected Legislative Council, an Executive Council chosen by the leader of the majority party in the legislature, the introduction of the ministerial system, and the abolition of the governor's reserve powers. In short, the demand was for representative and responsible government. The colonial administration, alarmed by the growing support for the PUP, retaliated by attacking two of the party's chief public platforms. The governor dissolved the Belize City Council in July on the pretense that it had shown disloyalty to the royal family by refusing to hang a picture of the King, and in October the four publishers and owners of the *Billboard*, including Leigh Richardson and Philip Goldson, were charged with sedition. Richardson and Goldson were convicted and sentenced to twelve months' imprisonment with hard labor and two more years on good behavior. A few days after their imprisonment John Smith resigned from the leadership and membership in the PUP. The removal of three of the party's four chief leaders was a blow to the party, but it left George Price in a powerful position.

In 1952, Price comfortably topped the polls in the Belize City Council elections, gaining almost twice as many votes as Smith, who stood as an independent. Within two years of its formation, despite persecution and division, the PUP was clearly a force with which to reckon, and Price was its leader. The GWU, which, unlike the PUP, had branches in all the districts at that time, fought a long and bitter strike in late 1952 against the Colonial Development Corporation, the Public Works Department, and the Belize Estate and Produce Company's sawmill. By the end of the year, the PUP was firmly associated with the GWU on a national level as the champion of the people's cause. Price was then secretary of the PUP and president of the GWU.

The period between early 1953 and April 1954 has been described as a "prolonged election campaign" in which "the colonial government openly took sides in favour of the 'responsible' leaders of the so-called National Party against the PUP."[9] The National party (NP) consisted of members of the old Legislative Council, led by Herbert Fuller, but only two of their candidates were actually Belizean. It was characterized by a fanatical loyalty to the British monarchy and was supported by Anglicans and Methodists, and the upper classes of Anglophile Belizeans. The PUP, they charged, practiced racial and religious prejudice, was communist, and was pro-Guatemala. The PUP leadership was young and radical, and identified strongly with Catholics and labor, but it was certainly not communist. Philip Goldson, who visited Guatemala in 1951, wrote an article praising the achievements of the Arbenz government and comparing it with the detested colonial regime in Belize.[10] The PUP received limited financial support from Guatemala in these early days, but clearly the leaders perceived Belize as belonging to neither Britain nor Guatemala. The attempts of the governor and the National party to discredit the PUP on the issue of its contacts with Guatemala failed. When the voters went to the polls on 28 April 1954 with universal adult suffrage for the first time, the issue was really colonialism: A vote for the PUP was a vote in favor of self-government. On that historic day 14,274 people, or almost 70 percent of the electorate, voted: The PUP gained 66.3 percent of the vote and eight of the nine elected seats in the new Legislative Assembly. In Belize North, Price won 75 percent of the vote against Smith, and in Belize South, Goldson won 53 percent of the vote against Fuller, the NP leader.

TABLE 5.1
Percentages of Total Votes for Major Parties in General Elections, 1954-1984

Party	1954	1957	1961	1965	1969	1974	1979	1984
People's United Party	66.3	59.1	63.4	57.8	57.6	51.3	51.8	43.3
National Party	22.9	12.5						
Honduran Independence Party		17.7						
National Independence Party				23.2	39.4	39.8*		
Christian Democratic Party				11.4				1.4
United Democratic Party						38.1	46.8	53.3

*Includes votes for People's Development movement
Source: Government Gazettes, Belize City.

From 1954 until 1984, the PUP won every general election and most local elections, against several opposition parties. The PUP, unlike the NP, had from its inception sought support from a majority of the people. Its leaders recognized very early that their only hope of challenging the monopoly of power held by the colonial administration lay in mobilizing working people throughout Belize, not relying, as did the NP, on the Anglophile professional and middle classes and the support of the colonial government. Much of the PUP's activity initially took place in Belize City where a third of the population lived, and the GWU carried the message into the inaccessible districts. The party had no clear economic philosophy and carefully dissociated itself from communism.[11] What economic goals it had were expressed in terms of "distributive justice," to be achieved by "cooperativism" and "wise capitalism," the last concept being undefined.[12] The principal goal of the PUP for thirty years was to bring about the constitutional changes necessary for independence and to achieve these through "national unity." The need to develop nationalist sentiment in a wide variety of classes and ethnic groups, in rural and urban Belize, led to the creation of a typically populist party, whose policies and strategies were defined by a leadership elite with little real participation from the membership. These characteristics have had two persistent and long-term consequences: (1) a tendency to factionalism, as fragile alliances between leaders with very different goals and values fragment, re-form, and redivide; and (2) the tendency for the leadership to become older and increasingly out of touch with the majority. In a small country like Belize, politics inevitably is highly personalized, and factional struggles within or between parties are often characterized by strong personal loyalties and attacks. Hence, issues are often obscured by both hero worship and mudslinging.[13]

Personal vilification characterized the serious split in the PUP in 1956 and the general election the following year. When Nicholas Pollard was expelled from the secretaryship of the GWU for alleged peculation, he and Price formed a new trade union, the Christian Democratic Union, and retained control of the PUP. Richardson and Goldson broke away from the PUP, while retaining control of the GWU, and formed the Honduran Independence party (HIP). Though the poll fell to 53 percent in 1957 and the PUP's share of the vote fell to 59 percent, Price's victory over his former political associates was impressive. Price himself obtained 70 percent of the vote in his constituency in Belize North, and all the opposition leaders—Goldson and Richardson of the HIP and Fuller of the NP—were defeated. The PUP won all nine elected seats, and Price assumed leadership in the Legislative Assembly, with the post of member for natural resources. Within the next year, however, further crises shook the PUP, leading to more defections and a consolidation of the opposition.

During constitutional talks in London at the end of 1957, Price visited the Guatemalan minister to discuss the future of Belize. The British secretary of state denounced Price and broke off the negotiations. When Price was removed from the Executive Council on the grounds that his actions were inconsistent with his councillor's oath of loyalty to the Crown, a political crisis resulted. The governor summoned a British frigate from Jamaica and accused Price in a broadcast of preparing to sell Belize to Guatemala. Two PUP assemblymen defected, and early in 1958 Pollard broke with Price and was expelled from the party. The two opposition parties amalgamated to form the National Independence party (NIP), and, soon after, Pollard created a new party, subsequently called the Christian Democratic party (CDP). The attacks by the British government and governor on Price were designed to discredit him, but instead they made him the focus of events, and the attacks of his Belizean opponents gave the opposition the appearance of being largely negative. The anti-Price campaign, far from isolating and weakening him, left him in undisputed control of the PUP and able to concentrate his considerable skills with an audience on the anticolonial issue. In November 1958, just eleven months after Price was stripped of his quasi-ministerial office, the PUP won twenty-nine of thirty-three seats in seven municipal elections, and he became mayor of Belize City. The colonial administration's preoccupation with Price had backfired: By expelling Price from the council they had not dislodged him from the center of politics. The Legislative Assembly, with two official members, three nominated unofficial members, and two PUP defectors, was a largely unrepresentative body, but Price retained popular support. Nevertheless, at about this time, Price himself came to accept the British constitutional process of decolonization.

For the critical constitutional conference in London in 1960, a prominent Belizean lawyer, Harrison Courtenay, brought the PUP and NIP together in a united front (the trade unions were not invited to participate and Pollard, the CDP leader, chose not to). The constitutional advances achieved through this conference ushered in a new phase in Belizean politics, one less volatile and more distinctly structured along two-party lines, each party contending for a majority of the eighteen elected seats in the legislature. In the 1960s, the PUP and George Price, by then the unequivocal national as well as party leader, consolidated their power. The PUP's success in three consecutive general elections was over-whelming and resulted in its winning all eighteen seats in 1961, sixteen in 1965, and seventeen in 1969. In the 1961 election the CDP was destroyed and the NIP reduced to a nominated opposition. The successive defeats of the NIP resulted in a split in its leadership in 1969, when Dean Lindo formed the People's Development movement (PDM). Price promptly called a general election, and the two opposition parties hastily entered an alliance. The effort was in vain, and Goldson, leader of the NIP, was the sole candidate to beat the PUP. With the collapse of the West Indies Federation in 1961 and the British government's determination to hasten its withdrawal from the region and from colonialism altogether, the PUP's political strength and Price's aspirations had become respectable. The introduction of the ministerial system of government and Price's elevation to the status of first minister in 1961 and premier in 1964 helped consolidate the PUP's supremacy and simultaneously reduced the status of the opposition.

In the late 1960s a new generation appeared on the political scene, young people who could not remember a Belize before the PUP, who saw Price and his ministers as an aging establishment, and who were impatient for social change and independence. Young men like Evan Hyde, educated in the United States, and Said Musa and Assad Shoman, who became lawyers in Britain, were influenced by the political currents around Black Power and the mobilization against the Vietnam War. Although these young idealists were radicalized by such movements, they never became the racists and communists that they were promptly dubbed in Belize. For this younger generation, radicalism meant something different than it had to Price and his colleagues twenty years earlier, though both groups were inspired by ideals of social justice and both, ironically, were unfairly labeled racists and communists. The PUP government pursued a policy of development that depended heavily upon foreign investment, whereas the young students were learning that such policies would lead to increasing dependency and neocolonialism in a world dominated by the United States. The young radicals were also dissatisfied with the organization of the PUP, whose elite leadership controlled policy tightly. Eschewing the PUP and its loyal opposition alike, Hyde, Musa, Shoman, and others started an extraparliamentary opposition, using public meetings, demonstrations, and mimeographed broadsheets to mobilize people in activities ranging from breakfast programs for poor children to education about the consequences of cultural and economic imperialism. For a while in 1969 Hyde's United Black Association for Development (UBAD) and Shoman and Musa's People's Action Committee (PAC) combined in a united front. Although they succeeded in showing that discontent was considerable in Belize and a latent force among the youth and poor, these young radicals failed to organize it as a social movement and their efforts soon diverged. Hyde stuck to journalism with his newspaper *Amandala* and became associated with the opposition parties, whereas Musa and Shoman joined the PUP, where they now constitute its most radical wing.

In the 1970s, the PUP lost some of its popular support, though it continued to win the national elections. In part, this is a consequence of the more united opposition that has existed since the National Independence party, the People's Development movement, and the Liberal party merged to form the United Democratic party (UDP). In the general election of October 1974, the PUP's support dropped to 51 percent, and the opposition coalition received 38 percent and won six of the eighteen seats. The success of the PDM candidates led to their chief, Dean Lindo, becoming the leader of the UDP. The new party received most of its support in Dangriga and the Toledo District, but it also obtained 48.8 percent of the vote in Belize City to the PUP's 50.2 percent. Musa and Shoman were both defeated as PUP candidates in 1974 but were appointed as senators, and Shoman was brought into the government as attorney general. Although the PUP seemed able to co-opt some of its former critics and to remain a broadly based party under the consistent leadership of George Price, the UDP has had several leaders in the last decade. Dean Lindo, the lawyer who replaced Philip Goldson in 1974, was himself replaced after he lost his seat to Said Musa in the general election of November 1979. The new leader, Dr. Theodore Aranda, a Garifuna, was challenged by the more traditional middle-class Creole leaders of Belize City, who succeeded in replacing him early in 1983 with Manuel Esquivel, a physics teacher and former mayor of Belize City.

The disgruntled Aranda, representative of Dangriga, then formed the Christian Democratic party.

Though the PUP won the 1979 election with 52 percent of the vote to the UDP's 47 percent, it has clearly been losing support, especially among young people. The UDP, for all its changes in leadership, or perhaps partly because of them, appears new in comparison with many of the old, lackluster leaders of the PUP. Among the PUP leaders in 1984 were six men in addition to Price who have been national political figures for twenty years or more. Louis Sylvestre and David McKoy were first elected in 1957, C.L.B. Rogers (who retired from the cabinet on grounds of ill health in January 1984), Fredrick Hunter, and Guadalupe Pech were all elected in 1961, and Florencio Marin in 1965. The youngest leaders, Musa and Shoman, who have been in the PUP over ten years, are now in their early forties. In a young population, the PUP clearly has difficulty attracting new, young talent to its leadership.

Following a UDP landslide in the Belize City Council elections in December 1983, in which the UDP won all nine seats by a massive majority, and the resignation of Deputy Prime Minister Rogers on 6 January, Price announced a new cabinet. The loss of Rogers, who had been minister of defense and home affairs, necessitated some major changes, but, although the reshuffle gave more influence to the younger members of cabinet, Price still relied on his old loyalists. The fact that the position of deputy prime minister was left open after Roger's resignation indicates that no clear successor to Price was present in the party's leadership. Moreover, there is considerable factionalism within the party elite. One minister, Louis Sylvestre, led the Anti-Communist Society in 1980 and joined the UDP in attacking Shoman and Musa, and sometimes even Price, as the agents of Cuba and the Soviet Union. In return, he and his wealthy associates are frequently accused of corruption. Price, a shy, self-effacing, ascetic, and very private man, has tried to hold together this fragile coalition of people who are anything but united.

According to the Independence Constitution, each division must have between 2,000 and 3,000 electors. At the last election, on 14 December 1984, the number of representatives increased from eighteen to twenty-eight. At the last election 75 percent of the electorate voted, giving 53.3 percent of their votes to the UDP and 43.3 percent to the PUP—a crushing defeat for the latter, which retained only six members in the House of Representatives. Most important for the PUP's future, perhaps, was the defeat of Price himself by the UDP's youngest candidate by 570 votes to 876. Subsequently, the right wingers, Sylvestre and Hunter, were expelled from the PUP and in June 1985 formed a new party, the Belize Popular party. The future direction and leadership of the PUP remains in doubt. Manuel Esquivel, at age 44, became Belize's second prime minister, but it is still too early to predict precisely what changes his more conservative and pro-U.S. government will make in 1985 and the future.

Above all, this election shows that, thirty years after achieving adult suffrage, this new nation is committed to democratic procedures and orderly changes of government. Both parties draw their supporters from the various cultural groups in Belize, although cultural identity still affects, but does not determine, political allegiances. Increasingly, Belizean politics is likely to be influenced by outside political pressures and hard choices that can be more or less identified in a Left-Right spectrum, about the country's economic development strategy.[14]

GOVERNMENT

The Belizean Constitution was drawn up in 1981, a few months before independence, and passed by the National Assembly. The Constitution specifies certain rights and freedoms for the individual and additional rights for citizens. It also defines the structure of government. The Queen of England remains the head of state, represented by the governor-general. The first Governor-General is Dr. Minita Gordon, formerly a teacher and education officer, who was appointed on Independence Day. The functions of the governor-general, like those of the monarch she represents, are mostly ceremonial, and she is expected to be politically neutral. The real authority in Belize lies in the legislative, executive, and judicial branches of the state, that is, in the National Assembly, the cabinet, the courts, and local government institutions.

The legislature, called the National Assembly, comprises the House of Representatives and the Senate. At a general election, the representatives are elected in each electoral division for a term not exceeding five years. All citizens eighteen years or older are eligible to register to vote. The number of representatives is now twenty-eight, ten from Belize City and the rest from the districts. The House of Representatives is presided over by a speaker, who is elected by the representatives, either from among themselves or from outside the House. The speaker is a chairperson whose job is to ensure that the House rules and procedures are followed impartially. The Senate consists of eight members appointed by the governor-general, five of them as advised by the prime minister, two as advised by the leader of the opposition, and one as advised by the Belize Advisory Council (a body of at least six persons, appointed by the governor-general on the advice of the prime minister after consultation with the leader of the opposition, to advise the governor-general on such matters as the pardoning of a convicted person). The Senate's chief function is to consider and ratify laws passed to it by the House. It can delay bills by refusing to ratify them or send them back to the House with suggested amendments. The National Assembly may be dissolved by the governor-general at any time on the prime minister's advice or if a resolution of no confidence is passed in the House. At any rate, a general election must be held within five years, or within three months after the dissolution of the National Assembly, at a date set by the governor-general on the advice of the prime minister.

In this parliamentary system the executive arm of the government is the cabinet, whose composition is determined by the prime minister, acting as the head of the government. The prime minister is the member of the House of Representatives who is best able to command the support of the majority of the representatives, so he is normally the leader of the party that won a majority in the elections, though he was elected only by the voters in the particular division in which he was a candidate. The prime minister may organize the ministries in various ways, as well as choose the ministers who will head them and who together constitute the cabinet. Most laws passed in the House of Representatives originate in decisions made in the cabinet, and, since the cabinet is formed by members of the party with a majority in the House and Senate, such bills are generally assured passage. The ministers are normally representatives (or occasionally senators) and hence must answer to the electorate, as well as to the National Assembly and the prime minister, for the way they administer the policies made by the cabinet.

According to this so-called Westminster-Whitehall model, the public service employees are supposed to carry out the policies of the cabinet, as instructed by the ministers who preside over their particular departments. The function of the Public Services Commission is to regulate the service by appointing and disciplining public officials. As servants of the state, such public employees are expected to be impartial to any particular political party. There have been occasions, however, when civil servants in Belize have taken political positions. Since many are Creoles, favored in the past because the British preferred urban English-speakers, they became suspicious of Price's Central American orientation in the 1960s and favored the NIP. In 1966, the civil servants went on a politically motivated strike, and in 1973 the Public Officers' Union president, who has been a prominent opponent of the PUP, was forced to resign from the public service. The problem of the proper relationship of the public servant to the political process is not unique to Belize, of course, but it is doubtful whether a nonpartisan civil service can be successfully insulated from party politics in such a small society where roles and relationships overlap so frequently.

The Belizean judiciary is independent of the legislative and executive branches of government. The legal system is based upon English law and practice with some local modifications. The Supreme Court, the head of which is the chief justice, hears the more serious criminal and civil cases, as well as constitutional cases and appeals from the lower courts, called Magistrate's courts. A Court of Appeal may hear appeals from the Supreme Court, and in special cases further appeal may be made to Her Majesty in Council—the Judicial Committee of the Privy Council.[15]

Although Belize is divided into six districts, no administrative institutions exist at the district level. Local government instead consists of municipal and village institutions governed by laws that assign them powers and responsibilities. Their activities are with such local matters as sanitation, upkeep of streets and amenities, control of markets and slaughterhouses, building regulations, and land use. Belize City has a council of nine members, and the six town boards—those of Benque Viejo del Carmen, Corozal Town, Dangriga, Orange Walk Town, Punta Gorda, and San Ignacio—have seven members each. San Pedro, Ambergris Caye, recently declared a town, elected its first town board in March 1985. These bodies are elected by universal adult suffrage, in elections held every three years. In these elections, unlike in national ones, the municipality is treated as a single constituency; the voter chooses between all candidates and those receiving the most votes win. Aliens who have resided in the municipalities for at least three years may register to vote, though they cannot vote in national elections.

Most villages have village councils, consisting of seven villagers elected every two years, usually at a meeting, though the vote can be conducted by secret ballot, as in the municipal and national elections, if desired. The village councils, unlike the city council and town boards, have no legal status or function. They operate as semiformal community organizations in such matters as the allocation of village lots, sporting, educational, and recreational events and village upkeep, and as a lobby for various improvement projects. Since they frequently come into contact with their representatives in the National Assembly, even the village councils tend to be politicized in Belize and often operate as a basis for support or opposition for the representatives. Some of the Kekchi villages in Toledo District still have the alcalde system, legally defined in 1884, in which the alcalde, who is elected annually by the villagers, acts as a village leader and spokesperson and has the authority to punish offenders in specified minor cases.

The Belize City elections have been politicized for fifty years at least, and the various town boards and village councils have become increasingly involved in national politics, with local elections fought along party lines. In fact, the extension of democracy to this level, which occurred in 1955, has given many Belizeans considerable practice in democratic political processes and may be one reason why the system has worked so well, so quickly. It can also lead to conflicts, especially over the distribution of jobs and resources, when the local government body is run by the party in opposition to the national government. Often the local government campaigns are treated as a prelude to the next general election and as an apprenticeship for aspiring politicians.

THE GUATEMALAN CLAIM AND INDEPENDENCE

The goal of the nationalist movement in Belize, from at least as early as 1940 and consistently after 1950, has been independence. The two obstacles to Belize gaining independence were the reluctance of Britain to allow Belizeans to govern themselves until the early 1960s and the complete intransigence of Guatemala, which has had a long-standing claim to the entire territory and has repeatedly threatened to use force. By 1961, Britain was willing to let Belize become independent and, after 1964, controlled only the defense, foreign affairs, internal security, and terms and conditions of the public service. Of course, the last sphere of authority that a colonial power concedes is always foreign affairs—it can hardly be otherwise by any definition of colonialism. Yet the British government allowed the Belize government to internationalize its case for independence after 1975 so that Belizeans participated in international relations even before their country became a sovereign nation. The reason for this was the stalemate in the protracted negotiations between Britain and Guatemala over the future status of Belize.

The origins of the dispute can be found in the eighteenth-century treaties between Britain and Spain in which Britain acceded to Spain's assertion of sovereignty over a sparsely settled and very ill-defined area. In the last of these treaties, at the Convention of London in 1786 British settlers were allowed to cut logwood and mahogany, but not to establish plantations, in the area between the Rio Hondo and the Sibun River. The British were not allowed to erect fortifications or to establish a formal government, though they did send a superintendent, part of whose function was to enforce the terms of the treaty. The last time that Spain attempted to take the area by force it was defeated at the battle of St. George's Cay in 1798, but in 1802 at the Peace of Amiens, which provided for the mutual restoration of conquests between Britain and Spain, Belize was not mentioned. Nor was there any mention of Belize in the treaty of 1814. The last time that Spain referred to the issue seems to have been in 1816, when it protested against the erection of fortifications at Belize.

After Spain lost control of the region in 1821, the British government still behaved as though the 1786 treaty was in effect and did not assert British sovereignty over Belize. Nevertheless, Britain frequently violated the terms of that treaty and extended its control over Belize, albeit informally and unsystematically. Thus, from 1797 a garrison and fortifications were continually maintained in Belize; in 1817 the superintendent was empowered to grant unclaimed land as though it was Crown land; and in 1819 Parliament passed an act providing for the trial of criminal cases in Belize. As formal government increased so did settlement. Settlers were occupying land as far south as Deep River by 1799, were at the Moho River by 1814, and had reached the Sarstoon River, the present southern boundary, by 1824. Certainly by the 1830s the Colonial Office regarded the entire territory between the Rio Hondo and the Sarstoon River as British and ignored the old ban on the cultivation of plantation crops. Thus, by the 1840s Belize was effectively a British colony, and, though Britain had never formally renegotiated the 1786 treaty with Spain, Spain had never attempted to reclaim the area or reassert its sovereignty.

The independent republics that emerged from the disintegrating Spanish empire in the 1820s claimed that they inherited the sovereign rights of Spain within the area corresponding to the previous colonial jurisdiction, a legal doctrine that Britain has never accepted. On this basis both Mexico and Guatemala, the latter becoming an independent republic when the Central American Federation broke up in 1839, have asserted claims to Belize. Mexico once claimed the portion of Belize north of the Sibun River but dropped this claim in a treaty with Britain in 1893 when it accepted the present boundaries. Since then Mexico has stated that it would revive its claim only if the Guatemalans were successful in obtaining the whole or a part of Belize. Mexico, pointedly, was the first nation to recognize Belize as an independent country and to support its application for membership to the United Nations. Guatemala, on the contrary, persists in its claim to the territory.

At the center of the dispute is the 1859 treaty between Britain and Guatemala. The British, having agreed with the United States in the Clayton-Bulwer Treaty of 1850 to refrain from occupying, fortifying, or colonizing any part of Central America, considered the Belize settlement exempt because it was a prior settlement. Britain created a formal constitution for Belize in 1854 and validated the laws of the settlement in 1855. Subsequently, in three treaties Britain handed over the Mosquito Shore to Nicaragua and Ruatan to Honduras and defined the boundaries between Belize and Guatemala. From the British viewpoint the treaty of 1859 did nothing more than settle the boundaries of an area already under British dominion, but the Guatemalans later developed the view that this was a treaty of cession in which Guatemala would give up its territorial claims only upon certain conditions and that it did not recognize British sovereignty over Belize. The Guatemalans consented to the treaty because the parties agreed "conjointly to use their best efforts" to build a road from Guatemala to the Caribbean coast, which Britain considered merely a favor to Guatemala that could benefit mutual trade.[16] The British did not consider that they gained any concessions or titles from Guatemala from the treaty, nor apparently did the United States, as any such gains would clearly have violated the Clayton-Bulwer Treaty. In 1863 an Additional Convention was signed in which the two parties defined more precisely each one's responsibilities for building the road, but Guatemala did not ratify the convention within the agreed period and then Britain said it was too late. When Guatemala protested that it would thereby lose its compensation, Britain denied that this was a valid interpretation of the 1859 treaty. Britain's position after 1857 was that, by surveying the road in 1860 and negotiating the Additional Convention in 1863, it had discharged its obligations to use its "best efforts" as required under Article 7, and so Britain refused to reconsider the matter. Guatemala threatened to repudiate the entire treaty in 1884, but did not do so in fact, and its subsequent actions have implied that Britain is still obliged to comply with Article 7 and hence that Guatemala still considers the treaty in force.

The whole dispute appeared to be forgotten until the 1930s when Britain sought Guatemalan cooperation in demarcating the boundary and Guatemala refused on the grounds that Britain had never helped build the road. In 1936, Britain offered £50,000 to help construct the road without admitting any liability, and Guatemala demanded £400,000. When Britain rejected that demand, Guatemala started making even less acceptable territorial claims. Britain offered to put the matter before the Court of International Justice at the Hague, but Guatemala rejected arbitration and declared that, as she considered the 1859 treaty invalid, she was entitled to recover the territory. In the Constitution of 1945, Guatemala stated that Belize was the twenty-third department of Guatemala. Since 1954, nationalist sentiment has frequently been whipped up in Guatemala—generally to divert attention from domestic problems—and the country has massed troops on the border several times in recent years.

Talks between Britain and Guatemala about the Belize dispute began again in 1961, but the elected representatives of the Belizean people had no voice in these negotiations. Meanwhile, Price, as first minister, achieved associate member status for Belize in the United Nations' Economic Commission for Latin America during a visit to Chile in 1961. On his return journey he visited Guatemala, where President Ydigoras Fuentes invited him to make Belize an "associate state" of Guatemala. Price refused and reiterated his goal of leading Belize to independence as a sovereign state. Fuentes later claimed that the resumption of negotiations with Britain in 1962 resulted from pressure by the United States on Britain, as part of a deal with Guatemala in return for the use of Guatemalan territory to train insurgents for the invasion of Cuba. In these unpromising circumstances Britain first allowed members of the PUP government to be present at the talks.

Between 1962 and 1975 numerous secret talks were held with Belizeans as observers, but all were fruitless. The Guatemalans often broke off negotiations and sometimes ruptured diplomatic relations with Britain and threatened war, as in 1963 and 1972. In 1965, Britain and Guatemala agreed to have a U.S. lawyer, Bethuel M. Webster, appointed by President Johnson, mediate the dispute. His report, presented as a draft treaty, proposed giving Guatemala so much control over Belize (including over internal security, defense, and external affairs) that Belize would be no more, and probably less, independent of Guatemala than it was of Britain. Though the United States supported the proposals, probably because of its anxiety about the leftist rebels in northeastern Guatemala, they were denounced and rejected by all parties in Belize. Price seized the initiative again by demanding independence from Britain, with appropriate defense guarantees.

A series of meetings between 1969 and 1972, five of them at ministerial level, was abandoned when Guatemala massed troops on the border and the British responded by sending a fleet led by the aircraft carrier HMS *Ark Royal* and several thousand soldiers. Guatemala declared that negotiations regarding Belize were indefinitely suspended, and Britain increased the size of its regular garrison. Talks resumed again between 1973 and 1975, but, when the Guatemalan proposal of ceding the land south of Monkey River was rejected, tensions flared again. Guatemala once more threatened invasion and Britain sent a squadron of Harrier jets to Belize. At this point the Belizean government decided on a new strategy—to internationalize the problem by taking the case for Belizean self-determination to various international forums. The government felt that by gaining international support Belize could strengthen its own position and weaken Guatemala's, while making it harder for Britain to make any concessions.

It was a reasonable assumption that most countries that knew nothing of Belize or the dispute would tend to side with Guatemala because the latter seemed to be trying to recover territory lost to a colonial power in the nineteenth century. Belize argued that its legitimate aspirations to independence were being frustrated by Guatemala, which was pushing an anachronistic and irrelevant claim to disguise its own colonial ambitions. For the Belizeans the issue was not the interpretation of eighteenth-century treaties between Britain and Spain or an unratified nineteenth-century treaty between Britain and Guatemala, but simply the right of the Belizean people to self-determination and independence. Between 1975 and 1981 this case was vigorously argued by such government leaders as Price, Rogers, Courtenay, and Shoman in such places as the Heads of Commonwealth Governments meeting in Jamaica, the conference of ministers of the Non-Aligned countries in Peru, and the United Nations.[17] The support of the Non-Aligned movement proved crucial and assured success at the United Nations. At first, Latin American governments supported Guatemala, and in the first UN vote that affirmed the right of Belize to self-determination, independence, and territorial integrity, in December 1975, Cuba was the only country to support Belize. In 1976, however, President Omar Torrijos of Panama began actively campaigning for the Belizean cause, and in 1977 Mexico and some other Latin American countries supported Belize against Guatemala. When the Sandinista revolution overthrew the Somoza dictatorship in Nicaragua in 1979, the Guatemalan military government lost one of its chief supporters, and the Sandinistas declared unequivocal support for Belize. In each of the annual UN votes on this issue the United States abstained, thereby giving the Guatemalan government some hope that it would retain U.S. backing or at least neutrality.

Finally, in November 1980 the internationalization campaign succeeded, with the strongest expression of support for Belize at the UN and the complete isolation of Guatemala. In a historic vote, the UN passed a resolution that demanded the secure independence of Belize, with all its territory intact, before the next session of the UN in 1981. It called on Britain to continue to defend Belize and on all member countries to come to its assistance. One hundred and thirty-nine countries voted in favor of the resolution, including the United States for the first time, with seven abstentions and no country voting against. Guatemala refused to vote.

A last attempt was made to reach an agreement with Guatemala prior to the independence of Belize. At prolonged talks in London under the chairmanship of Lord Carrington, then the British foreign secretary, Price and Shoman took a determined stand and would make no concessions. Guatemala dropped its demand for mainland cession and agreed to recognize an independent Belize with its existing borders. Eventually, in a face-saving formula Guatemala was given permanent and unimpeded access to Puerto Barrios through Belizean waters and the use (excluding military uses) of the uninhabited Ranguana and Sapodilla cayes in those waters. No question of sovereignty arose, as Article 12 made clear: "Nothing in these provisions shall prejudice any rights or interests of Belize or of the Belizean people." This ingenious package of proposals, called the Heads of Agreement, was initialed on 11 March 1981, but it provoked bad reactions in both Belize and Guatemala. The ultra-Right National Liberation movement in Guatemala considered it a sell-out, and the country refused to ratify the agreement and withdrew from the negotiations. In Belize, UDP rallies in its strongholds of Belize City, Dangriga, and Orange Walk turned into violent riots in which four people died, many were injured, and the property of prominent PUP leaders and their families was deliberately destroyed. The pro-UDP Public Service Union went on strike, and all public services and communications were suspended. Particularly vicious were the racist attacks from the Belize Action movement and the absurd slander from the Anti-Communist Society, providing between them

Independence ceremonies in Belmopan, 21 September 1981

the nadir of politically motivated violence and abuse in Belize. The British government declared a state of emergency, and by early April the riots ended. The UDP in fact had no real alternative to offer, and, with the prospect of independence celebrations in the offing, the opposition's morale fell. In summer it was announced that Belize would become independent on 21 September 1981.

The independence ceremonies and celebrations took place in a carnival atmosphere, witnessed by prominent leaders and diplomatic representatives from all over the world and the whole political spectrum. Delegations from twenty-six Commonwealth countries and thirty-five other countries, including Cuba and the United States, China and Canada, Nicaragua and El Salvador, Grenada and Jamaica, joined with musicians and dancers to celebrate. Belize promptly became the one hundred and fifty-sixth member of the United Nations and the ninety-sixth member of the Non-Aligned movement. But Guatemala is still not reconciled to Belize's independence, so a British garrison remains to strengthen the tiny Belize Defense Force, founded in 1978. In 1982, a military agreement was signed with the United States and U.S. troops might be stationed in Belize if the British withdraw. Meanwhile, post-independence talks between Belize and Guatemala have broken down. In 1985 there are signs that the Guatemalan constituent assembly is advocating a more flexible position on Belize, but the government continues to block Belize's entrance into the Organization of American States, the Inter-American Development Bank, and other regional organizations. Though Belize is now independent, it remains in an insecure position, threatened by Guatemala and in danger of being drawn into the increasing regional conflict.

INTERNATIONAL RELATIONS

Belize has been in the unusual position of developing its international relations while still a colony. Indeed, since 1975 Belize's strategy of internationalizing its problem was a crucial part of the struggle for independence. But only since 1981 has Belize been able to participate in international affairs and organizations with all rights of a sovereign state. That it has done so at a time of global recession and of increasing regional conflicts has posed some tricky dilemmas for those who shape the new nation's foreign policy.

Officially, Belize's foreign policy is one of nonalignment, while "recognizing our special ties with the United States of America as the leader of this hemisphere,"[18] which sounds rather like having one's cake and eating it too. What it means is that Belize is determined to stay neutral in the regional conflict while trying not to alienate the most powerful country in the hemisphere. Thus, Price refused to join the U.S.-sponsored Comunidad Democratica Centroamericana (COMDECA) but is willing to discuss Belize's military needs and even the possibility of having U.S. troops and bases in Belize with U.S. advisors. (For the United States such a development would enable Belize to be used as a base for action against the guerrillas in the Peten region of Guatemala, while ensuring that Belize itself remains securely under U.S. influence. To its critics, this policy not only smacks of neocolonialism but also seems to provoke further trouble by involving Belize in the dialectic of revolution and intervention.) While maintaining strong links with the Commonwealth, Belize is developing connections with other countries, such as Japan, France, and Mexico, partly to counterbalance the strong U.S. influence. France and Mexico have signed technical and cultural cooperation agreements, and the French ambassador indicated his country's attitude when he urged that "Belize remain free from the East-West antagonism and retain . . . its full independence."[19] The new UDP government is more distinctly oriented toward the United States and is trying to improve relations with such countries as Israel, South Korea, Haiti, and Taiwan, but it is too early to observe any consequences of this rightist foreign policy.

By its history, geography, and cultures, Belize is poised between the societies of the English-speaking Creole Caribbean area and Spanish-speaking Mestizo Central America. It cannot make a choice between these poles; rather, it needs to define its position and role in relation to them. Belize joined the members of the English-speaking Caribbean nations in an economic community in 1971, and several of these nations helped Belize in its diplomatic efforts to achieve independence. Sharing a common colonial experience and cultural attributes with the members of CARICOM, Belize will remain part of this economic integration movement while seeking to develop closer economic and cultural ties with countries in Central America, such as Mexico. Belize seeks economic and cultural cooperation with Guatemala, as it does with Mexico, and will persist in trying to resolve the dispute along the lines suggested by the Heads of Agreement. Another problem arises from the increasing U.S. military presence and intervention in the region—in the Caribbean as well as in Central America—which has resulted in narrowing Belize's political options and probably increasing Belize's dependency on the United States. Of special concern to Belizeans is the recent resumption of U.S. military aid to Guatemala, despite that country's appalling human rights record and persistent threats to Belize. A further problem, that is itself a byproduct of the escalating regional conflicts, is that Belize may become inundated with refugees with whom it is unable to cope, either economically or in terms of the strain they put upon the sensitive issue of race and ethnicity in Belizean politics.

If the Belizean economy fails to grow fast enough to cope with the expanding population and if this tiny country becomes embroiled in the problems of regional conflict and escalating U.S. military involvement, then its future will be a dismal one. In such circumstances ruthless and vicious people could relatively easily exploit latent racial prejudices that could tear the delicate national fabric apart. But such things do not have to happen. Belize has plenty of resources for a growing population and is capable of developing them for its people's benefit. With enlightened leadership, a viable path can be charted to keep clear of regional war, racist politics, and great-power conflicts. After centuries of colonialism, slavery, and exploitation, the people of Belize are trying to create, and surely deserve, a more just and humane society. The independence for which they struggled for over thirty years brings them a step closer to achieving that goal.

NOTES

1. Gordon K. Lewis, *The Growth of the Modern West Indies* (London, MacGibbon & Kee, 1968), p. 107.

2. Antonio Soberanis Gomez, "Memorial in regard to conditions in the Colony," to Gov. Sir Harold Kittermaster, 17 May 1934, BA, MP 700-34.

3. *The Belize Independent*, 26 March 1941.

4. Gov. J. A. Hunter to Lord Moyne, 24 October 1941, BA.

5. *The Belize Independent*, editorial, 27 August 1941.

6. A photograph of Price returning to a hero's welcome in Belize after a visit to London in 1957 shows a prominent U.S. flag alongside the PUP banner.

7. *Belize Billboard*, 3 January 1948.

8. See Assad Shoman, "The Birth of the Nationalist Movement in Belize, 1950–1954," *Journal of Belizean Affairs* 2 (December 1973):3–40.

9. Shoman, "Nationalist Movement in Belize," p. 22.

10. This was just before the democratic, reformist Guatemalan government of Jacobo Arbenz was overthrown by a coup, organized and supported by the U.S. Central Intelligence Agency, in 1954.

11. Defensiveness about charges of communism was probably exacerbated by the British overthrow of Jagan's government in

Guyana in 1953 on the grounds that he was about to introduce communism.

12. See article by Richardson and Goldson in Jamaica's *Daily Gleaner*, 5 September 1952, quoted in Shoman, "Nationalist Movement in Belize," p. 35.

13. Of course, I would not want to imply that such personalistic politics is confined to small countries, only that it is perhaps harder to avoid in such places.

14. See Tony Thorndike, "Belizean Political Parties: the Independence Crisis and After," *Journal of Commonwealth and Comparative Politics* 21, no. 2 (1983):195–211.

15. Created in 1835, this was an appeal court for the colonies, consisting of the British lord chancellor, chief justices, and other legal officers. Several other ex-British colonies have continued to allow certain appeals to this body.

16. Article 7; see L. M. Bloomfield, *The British Honduras-Guatemala Dispute* (Toronto, Carswell, 1953), pp. 103–106; D.A.G. Waddell, *British Honduras: A Historical and Contemporary Survey* (London, Oxford University Press, 1961), pp. 37–42; and J. Ann Zammit, *The Belize Issue* (London, Latin America Bureau, 1978), pp. 15–17.

17. See the Belizean government's publication for this campaign, *Belize: New Nation in Central America* (Belize, Cubola, 1975).

18. "The Prime Minister's Address to the Nation on Government's New Thrust for 1984," 17 January 1984.

19. *The New Belize* 12, no. 2 (February 1982):11.

Selected Bibliography

The books and articles selected below do not include official reports from government departments and commissions, many of which contain valuable information, and they are limited to publications in English that may be found in major libraries. In addition to these works, the general reader interested in Belize should seek three journals: *The New Belize*, published monthly by the government, the *Journal of Belizean Affairs*, published irregularly between 1973 and 1979 and reborn as the *BELCAST Journal of Belizean Affairs* in 1984, and *Belizean Studies*, published bimonthly by the Belize Institute for Social Research and Action (BISRA), St. John's College. Newspapers are generally poor in quality and short-lived, but the best was *Disweek*, which lasted from May 1983 to February 1985. (Articles about or relevant to Belize also appear in such regional journals as *Caribbean Quarterly*, *Social and Economic Studies*, *Journal of Caribbean History*, *Caribbean Studies*, *Caribbean Review*, and *New World Quarterly*.)

Ashcraft, Norman. *Colonialism and Underdevelopment: Processes of Political Economic Change in British Honduras.* New York: Teachers College Press, 1973. Less broad than its title suggests, this anthropological study of small farming and urban markets in the vicinity of Belize City is based on research conducted between 1965 and 1967.

Belize Today: A Society in Transformation. Belize City: Sunshine Books, 1984. An attractive, well-illustrated, and readable textbook for Belizean high schools.

Bolland, O. Nigel. *The Formation of a Colonial Society: Belize, from Conquest to Crown Colony.* Baltimore: Johns Hopkins University Press, 1977. The first detailed, scholarly study of the social and economic conditions of Belize in the eighteenth and nineteenth centuries that examines slavery and emancipation, and the rise and decline of the settlers' political economy.

Bolland, O. Nigel, and Shoman, Assad. *Land in Belize, 1765–1871.* Kingston: Institute of Social and Economic Research, University of the West Indies, 1977. Examines in detail the origins and development of the patterns of land use, the land laws, and the monopolization of land ownership. Includes a chapter on the legacy of this latifundia-type of political economy in 1971 and recommendations for land reform.

Buhler, Richard, ed. *Recent Archaeology in Belize.* Belize City: BISRA, 1976. Seven essays and a brief introduction on the important Maya archaeology in the mid-1970s.

Burdon, Sir John Alder, ed. *Archives of British Honduras.* 3 vols. London: Sifton Praed, 1931–1935. Extracts from the archives, prepared by a local committee under the governor's supervision, it is unreliable but useful on the earlier period of the colony.

Clegern, Wayne M. *British Honduras: Colonial Dead End, 1859–1900.* Baton Rouge: Louisiana State University Press, 1967. A well-documented study of economic and political changes in the late nineteenth century paying special attention to boundary questions, which makes good use of U.S. sources, by a professor of history at Colorado State University.

Dobson, Narda. *A History of Belize.* London: Longman, 1973. A good, readable summary by a British historian.

Edgell, Zee. *Beka Lamb.* London: Heinemann, 1982. A pioneering Belizean novel about the life of a girl, her family, and friends in Belize City in the 1950s; skillfully portrays the relations of church and school and the stirrings of politics in the colony.

Grant, C. H. *The Making of Modern Belize: Politics, Society and British Colonialism in Central America.* Cambridge: Cambridge University Press, 1976. A detailed, well-documented, and scholarly study that focuses on Belizean politics from 1950 to 1974, by a Guyanese political scientist who is now a diplomat.

A History of Belize: Nation in the Making. Belize City: Sunshine Books, 1983. An attractive, profusely illustrated textbook for junior high schools.

Humphreys, R. A. *The Diplomatic History of British Honduras: 1638–1901.* London: Oxford University Press, 1961. The standard work, thoroughly documented, on the relations between Britain and Spain in the early years of the settlement and between

Britain and Belize's neighbors in the nineteenth century, by a professor of Latin American History at the University of London.

Jones, Grant D. *The Politics of Agricultural Development in Northern British Honduras.* Winston-Salem, N.C.: Wake Forest University, 1971. A study of the cultural ecology and politics of the Corozal region from 1848 to 1968, with particular attention to the adaptations to sugarcane production, by a professor of anthropology at Davidson College.

Jones, Grant D., ed. *Anthropology and History in Yucatán.* Austin: University of Texas Press, 1977. Ten articles and an introduction on Maya history, three of which are about Belize.

Kerns, Virginia. *Women and the Ancestors: Black Carib Kinship and Ritual.* Urbana: University of Illinois Press, 1983. A fine anthropological study of ancestral rituals and kinship among the Garifuna in Belize, that shows the importance of older women and the mother-daughter relationship.

Land in British Honduras: A Report of the British Honduras Land Use Survey Team. London: H.M.S.O., 1959. An excellent study, broader in scope than its title suggests.

Lewis, Gordon K. *The Growth of the Modern West Indies.* London: MacGibbon & Kee, 1968. An encyclopedic account of the rise of nationalism and emergence of independence in the British West Indies, including a chapter on Belize, by a distinguished British political scientist at the University of Puerto Rico.

Lowenthal, David. *West Indian Societies.* New York: Oxford University Press, 1972. A comprehensive account of West Indian cultures and societies that includes information on Belize, by a distinguished geographer.

Minkel, Clarence W., and Alderman, Ralph H. *A Bibliography of British Honduras, 1900–1970.* A useful, though now dated, list of several hundred publications about physical, cultural, economic, political, and general aspects of Belize.

Shoman, Assad. "The Birth of the Nationalist Movement in Belize, 1950–1954." *Journal of Belizean Affairs* 2 (December 1973):3–40. The first detailed study of the early years of the People's United party. The author, a Belizean lawyer with qualifications in international relations, was a minister in the PUP government from 1974 to 1984.

Taylor, Douglas M. *The Black Carib of British Honduras.* New York: Wenner-Gren Foundation, 1951. A pioneering anthropological study.

Thompson, J. Eric. *Ethnology of the Mayas of Southern and Central British Honduras.* Chicago: Field Museum of Natural History, 1930. Study of the Maya of San Antonio in Toledo and Socotz in Cayo, based on field work conducted in 1927–1929, but still useful.

Thompson, J. Eric S. *The Maya of Belize: Historical Chapters Since Columbus.* Belize City: Benex Press, n.d. (c. 1972). A pioneering essay by one of the greatest Maya archaeologists, but much more has been discovered since this was written.

Thorndike, Tony. "Belizean Political Parties: the Independence Crisis and After." *Journal of Commonwealth and Comparative Politics* 21, no. 2 (1983):195–211. A reliable account.

Waddell, D.A.G. *British Honduras: A Historical and Contemporary Survey.* London: Oxford University Press, 1961. A good general survey, similar in format to this book, but now very dated. Not only has a great deal happened since it was written, but also much more has been discovered about Belize's history.

Warde, Shirley A., ed. *"We jus catch um."* Goshen: Pinchpenny Press, 1974. Eight folk tales from Belize, transcribed from recordings, with a brief note on Creole.

Willey, Gordon R., et al. *Prehistoric Maya Settlements in the Belize River Valley.* Cambridge, Mass.: Peabody Museum, 1965. Report of a major archaeological investigation.

Woodward, Ralph Lee. *Belize.* Oxford: Clio Press, 1980. The best recent bibliography.

Zammit, J. Ann. *The Belize Issue.* London: Latin America Bureau, 1978. A brief and readable summary of the dispute with Guatemala that looks at the historical background and the various arguments before urging that Belize should become independent.

Acronyms

BELCAST	Belize College of Arts, Science and Technology
BSI	Belize Sugar Industries
CARICOM	Caribbean Community
CARIFTA	Caribbean Free Trade Area
CDP	Christian Democratic party
COMDECA	Central American Defense Council
DFC	Development Finance Corporation
EEC	European Economic Community
GDP	gross domestic product
GNP	gross national product
GWU	General Workers Union
HIP	Honduran Independence party
IMF	International Monetary Fund
LUA	Labourers and Unemployed Association
NIP	National Independence party
NP	National party
PAC	People's Action Committee
PDM	People's Development movement
PUP	People's United party
REAP	Relevant Education for Agriculture and Production
UBAD	United Black Association for Development

UDP   United Democratic party
UNESCO   United Nations Educational, Scientific, and
               Cultural Organization
UNICEF   United Nations International Children's
               Emergency Fund

Index